LIGHT

OF

LIGHT

The life of a Healer and Exorcist

GARO DEDEYAN

CONTACT

✉ garo@lightoflight.co.uk

🅕 garodedeyanauthor

Acknowledgments

I would like to express my special thanks of gratitude to:

Susan Strecker

My editor who offered me invaluable help and guidance

Ryan Biore Lause

Cover design (ryanurz@gmail.com)

Hammad Khalid

Typesetting and formatting

Hmdgfx.com

The Light of Light volunteers

Paula Barder

"I wouldn't be the person that I am today without your help"

Claudine my wife and best friend

Disclaimer

This book details the author's personal experiences with and opinions about Spiritual Healing and Exorcism. The author is not a healthcare provider.

The author and publisher are providing this book and its contents on an "as is" basis and make no representations or warranties of any kind with respect to this book or its contents. The author and publisher disclaim all such representations and warranties, including for example warranties of merchantability and healthcare for a particular purpose.

The statements made about healing services have not been evaluated by the U.S. Food and Drug Administration. They are not intended to diagnose, treat, cure, or prevent any condition or disease. Please consult with your own physician or healthcare specialist.

Except as specifically stated in this book, neither the author or publisher, nor any authors, contributors, or other representatives will be liable for damages arising out of or in connection with the use of this book. This is a comprehensive limitation of liability that applies to all damages of any kind, including (without limitation) compensatory; direct, indirect or consequential damages; loss of data, income or profit; loss of or damage to property and claims of third parties.

In this book, the word patient or patients is used to refer to individuals seeking spiritual healing.

This book provides content related to physical, spiritual, emotional and/or mental health issues. As such, use of this book implies your acceptance of this disclaimer.

To my dearest daughter Taline...

"I hope that in the future, you will carry the torch where your mother and I have left off. Being in service of others is the purest form of love that we can express, and unconditional love is the closest that we can get to the blessed angels."

Introduction

My name is Garo Dedeyan, I am Lebanese Armenian and grew up in many parts of the world, embracing several cultures. I finally settled with my wife and daughter in London, England. My background is in Information Technology and I own an online company that provides internet services.

My life took different turns through the years and I went through many experiences that led me on my journey as a healer and exorcist.

People who would had once opposed me are now some of my most valued supporters, friends and patients. I am fortunate to be accepted for who I am and what I represent as opposed to being persecuted.

I have been of service to people from all religions and all walks of life, including scientists, doctors, psychologists, police, lawyers, etc.

From the poorest of the poor, the homeless and the destitute to the highest members of society—all who seek my help are treated equally, with no exceptions.

In writing this book I pray that readers are touched and that the content finds its way to enrich their lives.

All events in this book are real and based on real life experiences. This book is rated 15, parental guidance is advised.

CONTENTS

GREETINGS FROM THE OTHER SIDE...8

EYE SURGERY.. 29

MOVING TO A SCHOOL IN ENGLAND.................... 33

1986 – A DEAR FRIEND DIED IN MY ARMS................ 44

THE TURBULENT YEARS.................................... 60

MY GRANDFATHER AND HIS FRIEND 73

RUSSIA – EYE TREATMENT............................... 78

PATIENT R.. 88

PATIENT P. EXORCISM....................................... 109

AFRICAN EXPERIENCE 125

MAURITIUS... 132

PATIENT S. – BURNS VICTIM 139

REINCARNATION 147

INSIGHT INTO MY PERSONAL LIFE..................... 153

COMING OUT TO FAMILY AND FRIENDS 157

A CASE OF DEEP POSSESSION............................ 162

SOME OF THE DIFFERENT TYPES OF ENTITIES 173

THE SHADOW... 186

GOOD VS. EVIL.. 189

LOVE, HATE AND THREATS 193

THE HEALING PROCESS 203

DAYS AHEAD... 206

APPENDIX... 209

THE ENTITIES... 210

PORTALS... 213

EXORCISM... 217

ATTACHMENTS 221

DETECTION.. 227

HAUNTED HOUSES... 236

CURSES, SPELLS AND MAGIC.............................. 241

GREETINGS FROM THE OTHER SIDE

It began when I was eight years old. I was sleeping, and it was a quiet ordinary night. I woke and, raising myself slightly, rested on my elbows. My younger brother Andre was asleep in the bed across from mine and when I turned to look ahead and that is when I saw him; the little boy.

The child was standing at the corner of my bed on the left and looking at me. His eyes were piercing but friendly, and he beamed a large cheeky smile. He waved as if to say 'hello'. He greeted me with such excitement, it made me wonder who he was. I froze, not because I was scared, but because I was puzzled *How did he get in? Who was he?* At first, I thought perhaps he was a friend from the neighbourhood, but he didn't look familiar. I still remember his face—a bowl haircut, thin and friendly and a smile. In hindsight I think now that he was trying to play.

The child suddenly lowered himself and hid behind the corner of my bed. When I leaned forward to see where he had gone, he popped up and waved excitedly, grinning the whole time. I felt as if this 'child' wanted me to know that he was waving at me specifically to say hello—this was personal. He appeared almost translucent and it made me wonder. Although he didn't seem frightening, I was anxious because I couldn't explain his appearance. So I tucked myself under my blanket and eventually drifted to sleep. The next day I told my mother about my experience and she dismissed it as a dream, but I knew it wasn't. I was awake the whole time. I was not dreaming. I know what I saw.

I pressed my mother for answers, but I never got a satisfactory response. She was mysterious and dismissive, but that only made me even more curious to find out more about that night.Not too long after that experience, I fell ill with chickenpox and I was confined to bed. At some point, I woke up and saw an old man sitting on the chair near my bed. I did not recognize him, I was exhausted and unable to move. The old man smiled and seemed happy to see me wake up. I was confused as to who he was, he resembled my grandfather, but it wasn't him. I was too weak to think or say anything. I just stared at him. He leaned forward and extended his arm, then placed the palm of his hand on my face. His hand went towards my forehead and almost covered my eyes, it obscured my vision and I could no longer see him. He assured me that I would be fine.

"Garo ... Garo ... it's okay ... it's okay."

I remember his smile and hearing his voice clearly. I was not scared; on the contrary, I felt safe and comforted.

I recovered soon after that experience. The doctor told my mother I needed to rest because he couldn't explain how I got better so quickly. I did not tell my parents about the old man, for some reason, I felt that I had to keep it to myself. I could not explain what had happened.

At the age of twelve, when we lived in Qatar, I had similar experiences. We lived in a compound and my family often gathered in the living room to watch TV at night. I used to dread having to go to the kitchen, I always felt that there was someone there. If I was asked to fetch anything, I'd tip toe so as to not alert whatever or whoever was in there. Every single time I went in that kitchen, I felt scared and in my mind's eye, I saw an old woman out in the garden watching me. She had messy grey hair like a mane, bulging eyes and quivering lips. I felt she was trying to get inside, but something stopped her and she was trying to get my attention. She used to scare me and I never felt safe being there. I always ran back into the living room, about thirty meters from the kitchen and my parents never understood why I was always in such a hurry to get out of there. I'm not sure why I never told them, I think I was worried about being perceived as silly.

Unlike my previous harmless visitors, the old woman terrified me, and I dreaded the kitchen. I felt safer when I told myself she was a product of my imagination.

Fear played a big role in my early childhood, and I was subjected to it on many occasions. I was beaten on many occasions by a family helper who tried to intimidate me into not telling anyone what he did to me. I was scared to tell my parents lest he become more abusive. But they found out when they saw belt marks on my arm and shoulder. He was fired immediately but the damage was done—I stopped trusting grownups, especially men and I preferred the company of females. Unfortunately, I went on to experience abuse at the hands of several other predators who took advantage of me as a child. I had no way of knowing that what was happening to me was wrong, but I knew something wasn't right. When I grew up, I lived with the shame and the pain of abuse. It took years of therapy and healing to get over it. As I grew up, I met others who were once victims of similar ordeals and this gave me comfort knowing I wasn't alone. Abuse, fear and cruelty haunted me from a young age, but I never imagined how truly ugly and cruel people could be until later in my life when I started my healing service. I saw how rampant abuse really is and how widespread across all cultures and religions. Having gone through it myself, I learnt about the importance of other people's feelings and how truly delicate we all are.

Eventually my parents moved my brother and me to a school in Lebanon. It was the start of the civil war and the beautiful and magical Lebanon was quickly becoming an arena for anger and hate. I saw many sights a child should not see. I saw dozens of people lined up against a wall waiting to be executed. One day, when we were having some building works at our home, a car pulled out and four or more burly Christian militiamen went straight for the workers and started beating them with machine guns. I had never seen grown men being beaten before and their cries and pleas for mercy stayed with me for a long time. The workmen subscribed to an opposing political party and despite being Christian, they were not spared a brutal beating by Christians from a different sect. It was a painful sight for me to witness, I felt sorry for the workmen. Our neighbour came downstairs after the commotion and tried to assure my brother and me that it was nothing, and that they were friends and joking with one another. Adults make things worse for children when they lie or twist events, children are not stupid and I knew she was trying to cover up an ugly incident. The men received severe beatings and were bleeding profusely. I failed to understand how they were 'playing' with each other....

Despite all the changes taking place within me and around me and the raging war in Lebanon, I was fascinated by all things that were beyond the 'norm', the inexplicable and the bizarre. I read books, watched movies and documentaries on the 'strange' and the scary stuff. I didn't know the term for the inexplicable side of life was paranormal. I became more fascinated and drawn to the paranormal by the day and I soon discovered that some horror movies contained a lot on the subject so I started watching them.

My grandfather, a survivor of the Armenian Genocide, was a true Christian. He embraced Christianity and the Bible with great humility, and I respected him and loved him for his genuine faith. My brother and I moved to a different boarding school in Lebanon near my grandparents' home, and we visited them every weekend. I spent a lot of time with my grandfather, listening to him speak about God and Jesus. He never forced his religious beliefs or views on me or tried to convert me in any way. He shared teachings and stories from the Bible and I always listened to him with great interest, even if some of the stories appeared to be contradictory to the way Christians were behaving around us at the time. His faith captivated me and deep inside I felt connected to the saints and martyrs that he spoke of so highly. I knew it was all real and I had no doubt whatsoever about there being a larger purpose to life. Sometimes, unknown to my grandfather, I used to watch him pray. I always felt his energy, it was pure and calming. He usually prayed alone and in silence, he commanded respect because of his unwavering faith. I admired him, he was genuine and I learnt a lot from him. I observed everyone in our village treat my grandfather with great respect, they appreciated his sincerity and valued his beliefs.

His demeanour strengthened my faith and belief in God. There was no doubt in my mind that there was a God and that there was something far greater than us humans. My questions multiplied and I wanted to understand why things were the way they were, equally my faith grew stronger, I felt the connection to that which is greater in my core.

Our boarding school was run like a concentration camp, the teachers and supervisors resented the students and we hated them back. There was no warmth or love but strict rules, severe consequences and very hostile supervisors who were quite sadistic and enjoyed tormenting us psychologically and physically. Although the school was supposed to be Catholic, it was in fact faithless and cold, an empty shell full of pretence and twisted mentalities. I hated that school, it was horrible but we had little choice but to study there as our parents stayed behind in Doha to help secure our future. This was at a time when Armenians and Lebanese Catholics were at severe odds resulting hatred on both sides. Due to the fact that I was Armenian, I was picked on, bullied, beaten a few times and harassed. I could not stand up to my bullies because they were much older than me and so I sought refuge in the library. It was limited reading material because it was a religious school. Nonetheless, while browsing through the inventory, I came across a psychology book and in it I found an interesting section about mind over matter. I borrowed it from the library, and a few students and teachers asked why I was reading it. They were intrigued because it was not meant for my school year and not for a few years in fact. I made up excuses and kept it hidden.

Every morning before breakfast, we were marched into an exceptionally cold church for a short mass. It was chilly even on the hottest summer days. In hindsight, I wonder what energy may have lurked there. The service was monotonous and boring at times because of the daily repetition, but I really liked the hymns. The priest was solemn and intense, there was no soul in him as he droned away about us being sinners. I was not particularly interested in being lectured, besides, I couldn't grasp the concept of us being sinners since we were just kids and Jesus loved children. I often drifted away in thought, only to come back to myself at the end of the service. I remember feeling a warmth when I drifted away and it was only during these intervals that I felt something divine and beautiful.... I felt a connection to something that was higher, but it wasn't that church. My prayers were genuine, and I often knelt and prayed alone. In my mind I saw my grandfather praying alone at home. I was inspired by him. I felt my prayers were being heard because they were sincere. My soul longed for a deep connection and even when I lacked experience in all things, I felt the beauty of God and spirit.

A family friend used to visit us at boarding school and she often took us on days out. Once she took us to a bookshop that also sold gadgets and toys. I browsed for books, hoping they offered what the school library lacked. I quickly scanned through the books, trying to find anything connected to the paranormal. My eyes fell on a book in French, with a title that I vaguely remember as similar to 'Le Paranormal'. I opened the book and there were many photos and diagrams. I saw spoons being bent, people levitating, drawings of devils and saints ... there were so many photos that I could not fathom. I found the Holy Grail! This was exactly what I was looking for! So I dug deep into my pockets and came up with the money to pay for it. The book left me with hardly any pocket money for the week but I did not care. I desperately wanted that book!

I spent the next few weeks struggling to understand the French text. Even though I spoke and read French, it was a hard read and most of it I could not understand. Still, I was happy to be in possession of a book on a subject that fascinated me. The book went with me everywhere, and I read it at every opportunity, even under the covers in my bed in the dormitory, using a small torch light. I even read it during study time at school. I had no opportunity for privacy in the dorm room during the daytime or the library so study time was the best way to secretly read my book. I finished my classwork as quickly as possible and then opened my book concealed under other study materials and read. The book was simply magical and confirmed what I'd believed in all along; there were people with 'super powers'. I was mesmerised by the content and photos, and I wished had super powers! I discovered so many abilities and saw some incredible photos, some of them even scared me. I wished I could better understand, I struggled hard with that book. There was no control or age restriction at the time, but the bookshop shouldn't have sold it to someone as young as me.

One day, while seeking the attention of my peers, I proudly showed off the book to my classmates and I enjoyed their reactions. Of course, none of us could make much sense of the text but the photos were interesting enough to warrant a small crowd. I was taken by the 'wows' and seeing their reactions and it was a great feeling. The next day when I arrived at the study hall, I raised the top of my desk but my book was gone. I was surprised and rummaged through the limited content but I still could not find it so I panicked; who took my book and why?

Mr. Jamil, a hideous supervisor, pretended to be 'concerned' but was patronising. He smirked at me and asked what I was looking for. I explained that I couldn't find my book and that someone had taken it. He told me to ask the headmaster about it.

"Go on ... he's waiting for you and I am sure he will help you find your book."

I may have been a child but I was sensitive and I felt that something was amiss. I left the study hall, trembling slightly and I felt cold all over. I was aware of all the eyes following me as students turned their heads and looked on at me in contempt. They probably feared that I was to be severely reprimanded or punished as was the norm at that school, so they disassociated from me so that they didn't get in trouble. There was also the fact that the book was seen as 'weird' and it was implied that it was the work of the devil. Many who were excited by the photos the day before were now staring at me blankly as if I was the enemy. I was condemned and found guilty of something hideous, I could not fully comprehend why. The fear literally made me shake and I found the walk through the dark corridors to the headmaster's office painful indeed.

As soon as I walked in, I saw my book in the middle of his already cluttered desk. He casually picked it up and pretended to be leafing through it, momentarily ignoring me and pressing his lips firmly as if deep in thought while shaking his head and tutting to himself. Then he simply put it down and stared at me.

"Well Dedeyan, do you know why you're here?"

"I was told to come to see you, sir."

"Yes, indeed ... it is because of this book. Now, Dedeyan, are you going to tell me, who gave you this book? Don't worry, you're not in trouble, just give me a name."

"No one gave me the book, sir. I bought it myself."

"Where?" He looked disappointed.

"At a bookstore in the town next to our village."

He stared at me in silence, trying to determine if I was telling the truth.

"Who was with you at the time?"

"A lady friend of the family, sir"

"Does she know that you bought this book?"

"Yes sir"

"Did she not object to it?"

"No sir ... "

"How come?"

"I don't know, sir."

His anger was slowly turning to cynicism and in a patronizing tone he explained.

"Listen to me carefully, Dedeyan. This book, is not for you, it certainly does not belong here in our Christian school." He really stressed the word 'Christian'. "This book is the work of the devil! It is evil. You will never bring such books to this school in the future, do you understand?"

"Yes sir."

"We are a proud Christian school, we believe in our Lord Jesus Christ, everything else is insignificant. These things that you are reading are not from the Bible or the church. You will not read such things now or at any time in the future." He raised his voice slightly, his demeanour changed. "Do you understand?"

"Yes sir."

"You will not discuss such subjects with anyone in school or outside the school now and forever. These are matters that are beyond you and you will stop reading, asking and talking about these subjects.... Are we clear on this, Dedeyan?"

He pushed the now-closed book away with the back of his hand as if it contained a dead rat.

I'm fairly certain that a priest had told him about my inquisitive nature and my questions about religion and God. I never intended to be challenging or insulting in any way, quite the contrary, in fact. Yet, seeking answers did not appeal to an establishment that sought the mass production of clones who would never dare question its creed or dogmas in any way. I was a non-conformist and must have stuck out like a sore thumb. Any of the dozens of pupils or priests may have reported me. The school operated similar to a bee hive, if a hapless creature was to trespass into the hive, it would be dealt with severely.

I was lucky that I did not receive a beating that day. I do not know why I was spared. I had never felt more alienated in my life and as I walked from his office and to the study, I felt humiliated and defeated. Part of me wondered why I wasn't like the others. That book kept me interested in that soulless school and without it, I felt deflated and detached. I returned to study hall to hostile glances and stares by the other students. Who knows what had transpired during my absence and what the supervisor had told them about me. I felt an imposing hostility trickling and oozing from the higher echelons and now the other students considered me 'strange' and just stared at me. I did not fully comprehend their reactions at the time but I felt uncomfortable about being there. It was as if they associated me with something evil. I had become an outcast ... one of the damned ... a freak and so my persecution began. For a very short time, I very naively believed that I had made a breakthrough and made new friends. I was excited that we shared a common interest but later when the truth unfolded, I felt betrayed and ashamed because I came to understand that many of them were in fact mocking me to my face by pretending to be interested in my book. They were having a good laugh at my expense and I was too naïve to think otherwise.

In hindsight, I think that my educators were more afraid of the unknown than they cared to admit. Even though they themselves contravened many teachings from the Bible, they severely punished anyone who dared question their teachings or broke the rules. It was an atmosphere rife with double standards and hypocrisy. I hoped and prayed to be taken out of that school and far away from the staff and students. Years after we left, I learnt of widespread sexual abuse of students; luckily I was spared but they disgusted me far more than ever before.

I read the Bible to educate myself. The more I read, the more questions I had and the more I asked, the fewer answers I received. I came to the conclusion that the education system was narrow in vision and devoid of essential values. I was detached from the establishment and tried hard to belong but I couldn't. I was always the outsider in all things including sports and social activity. If a soccer team was chosen, I was the dreaded one nobody wanted. When a group of students were together and if I tried to join them, I would always feel left out because their tones would change. I found it awkward at times because no one seemed to want to engage in religious topics and I had little else to share with them, so I felt even more isolated.

In my heart, I felt that there was a different path ahead for me but I was in the dark and without any guidance, I had no idea what it was. As I grew older, I felt more distant from everyone around me. I saw my friends enjoying themselves with the lighter things in life; drinking, dancing, girls, etc. And there I was, thinking deep thoughts and trying to find answers to questions many kids my age would ever ask.

The loneliness was a torment that made me cry. I hated myself for being the way I was but I did not know how to change. I prayed for help and in prayer I found consolation. As I became more of an introvert, the older students picked on me even more. I endured even more bullying and physical abuse. They slapped me, tripped me when I was walking and pushed me when going past me. I suspected that at least one supervisor may have actually encouraged it, I caught him off-guard, he was laughing when a student unsuspectedly dashed past me and served me with a painful punch. Back then I used to wonder why I was being picked on all the time, I hated that school, I hated the students, the teachers but most of all, I hated myself. The fact that I was Armenian by origin, visually disabled being cross eyed and having been caught with material regarded as 'the devil's' teachings, these were all the ingredients for their hatred towards me. I have since forgiven the students because they were ignorant and fearful of the unknown.

I had an American teacher who was young and beautiful. I cannot recall her name but I shall refer to her as Miss Debbie. Many of the students tried to impress her by being 'cool'. Miss Debbie, brushed off advances politely by flashing a friendly smile. I liked her, I felt that she also liked me from the way that she spoke to me. To escape the bullies, I used to frequent the library and one day she happened to be there. I sat on a far corner table and she beckoned me over and told me to sit with her. I was extremely shy and nervous and I smiled back clumsily. I could not believe that she asked me to sit next to her when my classmates would kill for the privilege. She then enquired about what I was reading and I showed her a book on hypnosis and she smiled. She talked with me about the book and we were interrupted, a group of the older boys loudly walked into the library, and came straight to our table. I buried my head in my book, trying hard to ignore them. They struck up a conversation with Miss Debbie, speaking all at once, each trying to grab her attention. I knew that they had seen me but it was too late to avoid them and then their ridicule and bullying started.

"Hey freak! You ... yes you freak!"

They mocked me to Miss Debbie, laughing about me and as much as it humiliated and hurt me, I ignored them.

Miss Debbie told them to leave me alone and not to be mean. Eventually they left and I thanked her. She smiled back and said that it was okay. I was shocked that a staff member actually liked me and defended me. That experience moved me and made me feel appreciated, it gave me hope. It lifted my spirits, but it also made others jealous and with jealousy came resentment and even more violence.

As I left the library, I cried....

One day I was cornered by two thugs on the playground. They were much older and intimidating. The taller one, bent so his face was inches from mine, and insulted and threatened me while the other one laughed. He called me names and mocked me, I remember how his eyes bulged with hatred and I could not understand what I could have possibly done to him to warrant so much hate. He then mentioned something about my mother and it was offensive. In a flash, my arm went up and I grabbed his neck with my hand. He was not smirking anymore but choking and gasping for air, he was trying to clumsily move his arms about but it seemed as if my hand had latched on like a vice and it was squeezing the life out of him. I saw fear in his eyes and in his face. It gave me a lot of satisfaction. His friend did not come to his aid, he just froze and stared with his mouth open in disbelief. Suddenly I let go of his neck and took a step back. He was in deep shock and coughing and wheezing, then he stared at me and reached for his neck to feel where my hand was and began swearing. He grabbed my shirt, punched me and then pulled my hair, wanting to tear me apart.

"You tried to kill me, freak! How dare you even touch me?"

Interestingly, I did not feel any pain from that punch and whatever other beating I received after that. I had seen fear in the eyes of my bullies, and it was incredibly satisfying. I realized then that bullies and thugs hurt just as I hurt and they too were afraid, maybe even more so deep down but they dared not show it.

Another time, while wandering in a corridor leading up the classrooms, I was far away in thought and did not hear a supervisor call my name. I only heard him when he raised his voice and I responded quickly. I absent-mindedly replied "What?" It wasn't polite but I honestly had no intention of being rude, it's just that I was not thinking when I replied. The corridor was empty and he marched quickly towards me and grabbed my hair from the side of my head and shook me violently. He shouted in my ear, "What? What? What?" My eyes watered with pain from the assault. I tried to explain but he was so violent, I couldn't get a word in. Yet again I felt that I was being singled out and that his anger originated from hatred towards me personally. He walked off and left me hurt and in tears, I was in a lot of pain but most of all. I did not want to be at that school, I hated it.

If anything, I became more determined to pursue my path and learn more about the paranormal. My background at that school taught me a lot about how cruel and cold humans can be. Years later, I understood the nature and the origin of the hostility that was directed at me and why I was the subject of hatred. It was not all about me personally, but what I represented and what I stood for. As I became a practicing healer and exorcist, I learnt that people with underlying darker energies, find themselves reacting to me with inexplicable negativity or even hatred. I also learnt not to let it affect me personally but inevitably as a child, it did have a lot of impact on my life. It isolated me and made me more reserved and vulnerable.

Later in life I came to understand that the abuse I endured along with the bullying, were essential to my development as an exorcist. I had to learn how to stand up to the bullies eventually and to my abusers and from that my character grew eventually and I learnt how to confront the demons and entities. Some say that I was being prepared.

The few friends I made at that school visited me at home sometimes and we used to hang out and play. They were not close friends but rather more tolerable than the others. One day, we watched a horror movie. A character drew a pentagram on the ground, stood in it and summoned entities. My friends laughed and imitated the main character. I told them that I believed it was real. They roared with laughter and told me to stop talking nonsense. My brother was also in our group and I remember him looking, wondering. I told them that since they did not believe me, I'd prove it to them. I walked to one of the bedrooms, drew a similar pentagram and repeated the words I had just heard in the movie; I wanted to summon an entity to prove to them that what I was saying was true. I kept repeating the sentence over and over until it had become almost a mantra and I was lost in it. Then suddenly there was a shout from the living room where they were all gathered and someone called my name. As I entered, I saw panic in the room.

"What is wrong?" I asked

"Look!" one of them exclaimed and pointed to the chandelier.

It was swinging wildly from side-to-side and I assumed they were pranking me.

"You did this, I know you did," I said to the one who pointed out the chandelier and he quickly denied it. I asked him who did and they swore it was not them. I asked my brother and he said he same thing—the chandelier started moving on its own. Then the swinging stopped almost completely and the chandelier started shaking. The motion and behaviour changed right before my eyes so I knew it was not them. I too felt scared but I also felt empowered because I proved to them that I was right even at the cost of doing everything wrong.

We called it a night and 'escaped' from there. My friends descended the common stairs hastily and were keen to leave. My brother and I joined my grandfather, and the night's events were never discussed again. I did ask my brother in private if it was any of them who caused the chandelier to swing and he swore to me that it wasn't any of them.

A few days later I went to my family's apartment where we'd had the experience with the chandelier, and I felt uncomfortable. The sensation was similar to when I went in the kitchen when I was a child. I didn't know what was wrong but I wanted to be out of that apartment as quickly as possible. I felt that someone or something was in the apartment, unseen but lurking in one of the rooms. I got what I needed and proceeded to the front door. There I was confronted by a black cat and it hissed at me. Unlike other stray cats, this one did not flinch or try to escape when it saw me, it held its ground and looked angry. I quickly closed the door. Where did the cat come from, I wondered. The building's main door was always shut, how did it enter? I was feeling uncomfortable in the apartment and I really wanted to leave so I opened the door and the cat was gone. I went to the roof, but the door was shut and locked. So I went down the stairs all the way to the ground floor where the front door to the building was also shut. There was no trace of the cat, it had vanished. I kept thinking of the chandelier and associating the cat's visit to it.

It took a while for me to muster the courage to go back to my parents' apartment. It felt eerie for a long time and I continually felt the presence becoming more prominent. I felt guilty for doing whatever I did and for starting the sequence of events. I wondered what would happen when my parents come to stay, I was scared. The next day, I went to our apartment in the morning and opened the windows and shutters. I cleaned the pentagram that I drew on the floor in the bedroom and left. I returned a few hours later to close the shutters and windows and felt that the atmosphere had already changed somehow. I wasn't feeling afraid or nervous anymore, whatever was in the apartment had gone. In time, it was forgotten and the whole episode with the swinging chandelier was never mentioned again. This remains a mystery to me but I also consider myself lucky because whatever it was that I dabbled in that night, could have potentially become far more serious.

I did succeed in 'shocking' my friends into believing but I also managed to terrify myself in the process. This was my first lesson into not abusing my gift, but of course, I had a lot to learn. In years to come I failed many times as a result and for similar reasons. It was hard for me to resist the temptation not to use the gift to impress others. However, with age came awareness and maturity and in time I understood that the gift is independent of me and from a higher source, I am not entitled to it, nor am I able to command it to work at will. The gift is not to be abused for entertainment or curiosity, it is not to be challenged either. The gift should remain unadulterated and pure and that it operates for the specific reason of benefiting others.

Later in life I understood that I was not gifted but rather blessed to be chosen to serve. It took me a long time to understand the difference.

EYE SURGERY

When I was a child, I underwent a number of complex surgical procedures to my eyes. I suffer from extreme strabismus, a vision disorder where the eyes are unable to co-ordinate and work together. The old school of thought was to treat all sufferers with surgery, which in my case proved to be, in fact, detrimental.

Medicine and technology were primitive back then, laser was only mentioned in science fiction movies and even then, it was a subject of ridicule. Surgeons were devoid of feeling and completely detached from their patients. I was probably only twelve at my first eye surgery and I remember being on the cold leather operating table being put to sleep, terrified at my predicament and completely at a loss. I could not even comprehend English or speak it well enough to understand what the grownups in scary surgical masks were talking about. They went on with their business as if I wasn't there and only spoke to me when it was time for me to count back from ten.

The aftermath of the surgeries was painful. My eyes were

shut for weeks and I was completely blind during that time. I used to wonder if I'd ever open my eyes and see again. Being in the dark is a horrible feeling. I could only hear and feel the touches of my loved ones. I couldn't reach for water or eat from a plate.... It was isolating, intimidating and scary. My dear mother stayed with me in the hospital in London during these times. She used to feed me, clothe me and help me cope. Her English was extremely limited and she fought against ghastly nurses. My father was in charge of my younger brother and they darted back and forth between the hospital and the hotel. This was an important time as I bonded with my mother, in the dark, her voice was magical in my ears. Her touch warm and loving, she made the pain go away.

After the second surgery, I was assigned to a room in the children's ward, but it was close to the adults' section. I was without sight and got used to the children playing in the ward, singing along to nursery rhymes and playing with their toys. I so much wanted to play with them but I could not, I was confined to bed, alone, in the dark. My mother was not with me at the time. One night, when alone and unable to sleep, I listened to the deep painful moans of an elderly gentleman who probably had gone through a painful surgery himself. They were long, eerie haunted groans, akin to the sounds that stereotypical ghosts make. I lay frozen in bed, scared from the sound, unable to do anything. I spent the better part of that night awake, blind and in the dark and in fear of the haunting voices.

I will spare the reader gruesome details of how crudely the nurses dressed my injuries and how they forced open my eyes. The thought now makes me shudder and I remember the warm trickling of blood on my face as they pinned me down to stop my struggle and my muffled agonised screams and used their hands to pry open my eyes.

As a child, in fear and in pain, all I was concerned about was going home. Little did I know back then that my painful experiences would build my character and teach me to trust my core senses. The darkness that I feared and which was my enemy would became my friend as it taught me to be in control over my senses in the face of fear. As I grew older I found myself 'feeling' or 'sensing' situations and people, my perception changed and became greatly heightened. What was once a nightmare turned out to be a blessing. I conquered a part of my fear at an early age.

It was yet again my preparation for my task ahead. It made me more in tune to my senses and heightened them.

I briefly touched a reality that many of us fear and would not even wish upon our enemies—I experienced blindness. In doing so I learnt how fortunate I am because despite my visual disability, at least I can see. My predicament was temporary, I eventually regained my vision but the blind do not. I salute their courage and admire their determination.

My brief venture into the 'dark' taught me a lot about myself and life. I interacted with people while I was blind so I had to rely on my senses. One of my most valuable observations was that a large majority of people lead their lives with open eyes but they are unable to see, for in spirit they are completely blind.

During my second operation I woke up to find myself

looking at a nurse sitting in front of a set of vertical dials and monitors and taking notes. I tried to say something but I could not, I found it strange that I could not speak so I tried to get the nurse's attention by flailing my arms but she never looked at me. Suddenly, it dawned on me that I was looking at the nurse from an angle that was far higher than I'd ever been; I was in fact looking down at her, as if I had risen high up near the ceiling. When I wondered what was going on, in a flash, I could no longer see the nurse, I felt the bandages on my eyes and I was in darkness again because my eyes were shut, how could it have happened? I kept thinking about it even while being wheeled back to my hospital bed, I had seen her and I was not dreaming. What was even stranger was the fact that I saw her from a vertical angle, looking down at her, which meant that I was standing up. How could I have been standing up and looking down at the nurse when I was actually lying down and my eyes bandaged.

Later, I discovered, that I was not alone and others have experienced similar experiences, many of which were far more profound than mine. I have had various explanations about my experience, ranging from a dream state induced by the withdrawal process from the anaesthetic in the recovery room to a theory that my soul had actually left my body and that explains how I was able to look down at the nurse. It was not a dream, the sensation was totally different from a dream, I was fully conscious and in control of my faculties.

As for my soul leaving my body, it seemed to me the most plausible explanation after eliminating all other possibilities and who am I to disagree?

MOVING TO A SCHOOL IN ENGLAND

Due to the civil war in Lebanon intensifying and presenting a threat to our safety, my parents thought it best to send my brother and me to a boarding school in England. I hated my school in Lebanon and I wanted to put it all behind me, so leaving it was the easiest step in the world. Our new school was Lebanese located in Bath. Most students were in the same predicament as us. We were all sent away by our parents for our own safety, to be excluded from the war and the depraved divisive mentalities.

I was glad to be away from the boarding school in Lebanon and I looked forward to a fresh start. My brother and I didn't know anyone at that school but on the surface they appeared to be friendly. My brother settled in with his new friends, I unfortunately found it much harder to adjust and was to find that some of the ghosts of the past were back to haunt me once again.

Building work at the school was not yet completed, so

our dormitories consisted of rooms in porte-cabins. I shared a room with three other male students. Most of them knew one another from Lebanon. I was an outsider but I hoped that it would not be for long, some students seemed pleasant while others I immediately felt I should avoid, including some of my roommates. On the first day, I kept out of their way but when it got dark, we were sent to our rooms by the housemaster. I struggled to sleep that night, my thoughts wandered to my parents, the lovely memories of us fishing as a family or lounging at home on weekends watching movies and swimming in our pool in the garden. Boarding school was such a stark contrast to the life I was used to; we were innocent and played freely and I grew up to a reality where people respected and liked one another.

The room was pitch dark, I eventually drifted off ... but sleep was interrupted by a voice calling my name "Garoooo ... Garoooo ..." The voice was mimicking a ghost and it was one of my roommates. The others laughed and then they joined in by producing all sorts of sounds. They took turns calling my name using scary voices and it did affect me, I was afraid, even though I knew my roommates were behind it. At one point they all joined in and started laughing manically while calling out my name over and over again. I was shocked, I had no idea why they were behaving this way. I closed my eyes and prayed quietly, hoping that prayer would bring an end to the madness somehow. Eventually they got bored and we all fell asleep.

The next day, I tried to befriend whoever I could from my room but they were not interested, so I went on with my first day at school. The atmosphere was far less hostile than that of my previous school and the educators seemed to be genuinely interested. The students, however, were spoilt and took advantage of the fact that the school was not fully functional yet and ran amok.

I was busy all day at school and I forgot the episode from the night before. I assumed that perhaps things would be different on the second day. At the dorms I found at least one roommate being more communicative albeit in a limited manner but at least it was better than nothing. Unfortunately, that night was a repeat performance and quite worse than the night before. Shouting, screaming, scary noises and sounds and laughing like hyenas. Once again, I prayed and hoped that it would all come to an end but they just carried on. Eventually it got so bad, I was overcome with anger and I shouted "Enough!"

... silence ...

All the noises stopped, including the giggling and the laughter. They all went quiet, perhaps because they did not expect my reaction; I even surprised myself. That night was awkward and I felt unwelcome in the room, the atmosphere changed and things became more tense. They eventually started mimicking me and making fun of me again and it went on for a while. The next day I explained to the staff and asked to be moved to another room and they reluctantly obliged. I never knew exactly why those boys tormented me. Hindsight has taught me that perhaps they sensed my energy and were fearful of it and me.

I settled in my new room and made friends with my new roommates who were pleasant by contrast. The days went by smoothly and I found myself enjoying the school and my new friends. There were a few eccentrics around and I became part of their group. What also helped me greatly was my sense of humour and the extremes that I was prepared to go to, to make everyone laugh.

After a few weeks, I had a strange dream. I saw the figure of Jesus Christ in a white robe and for some reason I felt cold and scared. Suddenly, his face changed to that of a demon and his eyes bulged. The lips formed a strange shape and he smiled which made it look horrible. This was not Jesus Christ, not even a symbolic image of him. I sensed that this was an impostor and I was right. This was my first encounter with a shape-shifting entity.

"You are not him!" I shouted in the dream.

He looked to his side and shouted, "Get him!" I started running and fell down a ravine. I saw a bright light, like the sun but without the heat. It was blinding, I was struggling to see and that is when a hand appeared in front of my face and shielded my eyes. Then I heard and also 'felt' a voice in my core:

"You are safe ... don't be afraid."

The calming experience was profound and real in every sense, it was not a dream. The colours were vivid and the communication reached deep into my core and assured me. The voice was distinct and memorable. I never forgot that beautiful and gentle voice, not even now, thirty-six years later. It was the voice of my communicator with whom I now have the honour to serve.

When I am in service and in the face of the darkest of entities and demons, I hear the same voice and I am always comforted and assured.

"Pray Garo ... pray"

Praise and glory be to God and to his beautiful angels ...

Thinking back over the years, I now feel the impact that dream had on me. While healing is beautiful in every sense, exorcism can only be fulfilling at the end. The process is gruelling and a test of physical and mental endurance. Any assurance or support given is well received, especially if the source is from the heavens above.

As intense as that experience was, I soon forgot about it. I wanted to make friends, I was lonely and I struggled to be accepted. My new roommates were by far friendlier than the previous bunch but I still felt out of place because the majority of the students were spoilt and rebelling against the school and its staff. It was common for the students to destroy school property, to throw things at the staff and to be as horrible as possible. I found myself slowly imitating them, trying to impress them and I discovered that the more mischief I got up to, the more popular I became.

I must say that I am not proud of this chapter in my life but I guess that it is a part of me and I had to go through it to learn. I am ashamed to say that I went to extremes that left others way behind. I picked up bad habits, drinking, drugs, gambling ... anything bad and there I was. I lost myself completely to anything that took me away from my old self. I was lucky that I had some good friends but equally

I made some new friends who were rotten. I was caught a few times during my escapades, and I could always see the disappointment in the faces of my teachers and the staff.

"You are a good guy Garo, why are you behaving like this? I cannot believe that you are the culprit.... *You* of all people!"

These were sentiments often echoed in the headmaster's office and the detention halls. In addition to the fact that I wanted to be 'bad' to be accepted among my peers, I also had a learning disability which was later discovered by my now-wife Claudine; I suffer from dyscalculia; a struggle with numbers. I was once in math class, the teacher was explaining a formula and I just could not grasp it. I raised my hand to say that I did not understand, so he explained it again. Unfortunately, I again failed to understand and I asked him again. He repeated himself a few times and I still did not understand but I did not raise my hand again as I was too embarrassed. My classmates grasped it from the first time and there I was after five or six repetitions and still puzzled.

"Did you understand?" the maths teacher quizzed me.

"Yes sir."

"Are you sure you understood it?"

I was afraid that he would ask me to explain it, I was sure that he knew from my face that I did not understand. I was never a good liar ,so I sheepishly admitted that I did not understand.

"Oh for goodness sake! How could you not understand?" he shouted. Then he took a seat among the students and asked a female student to go to the front and explain it to me.

"I think I'd better sit here and let you explain it to the idiot of the class."

This was my turning point against education and the establishment. The ignorant fool who embarrassed me in front of my classmates could not look me in the eye afterwards. I wondered why I was different and why I couldn't understand the lessons like the rest of the class. I felt inferior and became even more distant. I lost my confidence and that gave way to bitter resentment because I felt that I was damned. A new conflict started inside me and I lost myself even more to drugs and drink and behaved like an imbecile for the remainder of my stay at that school. I was unhappy and feeling quite low most of the time. I had no idea what depression was but after describing my situation to the school doctor, he put me on anti-depressants. It is remarkable just how much of an effect teachers can have on their pupils, especially ones who are already on the brink. While the maths teacher flung me into self-doubt, other were supportive, even when I was nasty to them.

One of my inspirations was my English teacher, Mrs. Dew, she is the one who discovered my passion for reading and writing. It so happened that one day, I was alone in my dormitory room and I was feeling sleepy but I could not sleep. I tried to do homework but couldn't focus. I drifted but in a pleasant way. I opened a notebook and I started writing. I wrote some sort of poem. I am not usually a fan of poetry so I have no idea why I wrote what I did. The next day, I put the poem on Mrs. Dew's desk as a cheeky but amiable prank, I was fond of her. She walked in and glanced at her desk and before greeting the class, she picked up the poem and read it and then she glanced at me. I remember her face, she was blushing and in tears, her smile was radiant.

"I knew it was you, may I keep this?"

"Yes," I said awkwardly, not wanting to be the subject of attention. I wanted to be the naughty one.

The next day in Mrs Dew's class, I forgot the events of the day before and I was once again being the class clown or rather, the idiot of the class. Mrs. Dew asked me to stop it but I went on and on throwing things at my fellow students, making noises to distract the class and throwing objects into the corner of the room. It got so bad that eventually Mrs. Dew slammed her hand on her desk

"Enough! Garo ... stop it!"

She looked genuinely infuriated and I calmed down quickly, she had that effect on me. She stood up and opened the door, I thought that she was going to ask me to leave but she actually stepped out and asked me to follow her. She took me to several classrooms and in each one she showed me a photocopy of my poem plastered on the wall.

"I put up the copies so other students can enjoy your lovely poem. I even put them in the corridor."

I didn't know what to say. We walked back to my class and she asked,

"How can someone so sensitive be such a terror at the same time? Can you explain it? I'm so disappointed in you!"

I remained silent, she was right and I knew it but I was in shock about my poem being plastered everywhere and I was also quite ashamed of myself. When we reached my classroom, the other students looked to see if I was taken to the principal's office. They were desperate for a reaction. Instead, I sat quietly at my desk, lost for words. Over the next few days, various students and teachers stopped me to congratulate me on my poem, I felt overwhelmed on one hand, it was my greatest achievement but I also lost my 'naughty boy' status, which in hindsight was not a bad thing.

Mrs Dew introduced me to the works of famous writers such as George Orwell, Alan Paton, and Hemingway. She nurtured my passion for reading by buying me books to read in my spare time. I was absorbed in all the fantastic books and I read at every opportunity. She spent her own money and was delighted to see me so interested. One day she tested me to see if I was actually reading the books so she asked me to quote something out of Orwell's 1984 and I immediately quoted, "If you want a picture of the future, imagine a boot stamping on a human face—forever."

"Oh that's good! You actually read it.... Who said that line, Garo?"

I told her that it was O'Brien who said it as he was torturing Smith and she broke school protocol and hugged me. I felt her warmth and love and even now when I remember her, I struggle to hold back my tears. May her soul rest in eternal peace....

On our day trips to Bath, I headed to the bookstores and the paranormal section, where I spent time scanning books to satisfy my curiosity. On every trip, I ended up buying at least three or four books which I read very quickly. I had an insatiable appetite and curiosity about the paranormal. I had become quite obsessed by the subject. One of my roommates was equally interested in the subject which was rewarding as I finally found someone to converse with. We often shared different ideas and points of views, he introduced me to some of his favourite books and I shared many of my books with him. We spent some memorable times together. Unfortunately, my friend left a year later and I went back to spending time alone and away from the others. I missed him a lot, his stimulating mind and deep conversations, the majority of other students were shallow by comparison.

Most of my friends were girls. I preferred being with females. My knowledge of females was limited, I still felt a deep connection and learnt a lot from them. Years later I understood I was drawn to their sensitivity, sophistication and open-mindedness. Most of all, I felt safe in their company.

On the final day at school, the school ordered a few buses to take the students to London. We were all graduates and independent, we were finally free. Several teachers came out to bid us farewell, including the head supervisor who we had been unkind to. Tears streamed down his face. This was the man who I had been absolutely horrible to at times. I stood frozen, crying. I felt terrible for the grief I'd caused him and the other teachers. I was ashamed but too arrogant to apologize. I was torn but it easier to leave than apologize.... I left without even thanking them, I was such a coward.

1986 – A DEAR FRIEND DIED IN MY ARMS...

I was nineteen years old and attending college in London. I was scheduled to visit Lebanon in the summer of 1986. Prior to my departure, I was with friends in my apartment enjoying a lazy afternoon, watching movies and talking, when I found myself drifting. It was as if I was daydreaming but deeper. Then a sad feeling took over me and I could not explain why. It was a lovely afternoon, nice and bright, we were all in good spirits, so why was I suddenly so sad?

A friend expressed concern and commented that I was in another world and without thought, I replied that something bad would happen in Lebanon. After saying it, I snapped out of the 'daydream' but the feeling was strong. We enjoyed the rest of the afternoon and I did not give it any further thought. I eventually travelled to Lebanon and met up with my friends and was reunited with my dear friend Salim. Salim was the fiancée of my now sister-in-law, and we had become close, I saw him as my older brother. We spent a lot of good times together and enjoyed our mutual interest in wireless communication as radio amateurs. He introduced me to High Frequency Radio and showed me how radio amateurs all over the world communicated as a hobby. It was absolutely fascinating to me and I was immediately gripped by my new found entertainment.

One day, while visiting my sister-in-law, Salim asked me to join him at the radio room where he was engaging with several radio amateurs. My sister-in-law left us to go to work, so I ended up alone with Salim. We were both in the room for a few hours while he struggled with the Linear Amplifier or signal booster to make it work. He switched it on and produced a strong and scary electric noise and then switch off on its own. This was infuriating him because he was trying to communicate with someone and wanted the extra power to his signal. When I heard it produce that noise, it worried me that he was fumbling with the amplifier to make it work so I warned him and asked him to take care. Salim was fixated on the amplifier and wasn't paying attention, he got it to work eventually but by then I got bored and went downstairs to play the piano instead. On my way down I felt the urge to look back and I saw Salim looking back at me and smiling at me, it was a beaming smile. I smiled back and resumed my descent to the piano.

I barely started playing when the amplifier made a noise and switched off. Salim fussed and cursed and opened the cover to repair it. A few seconds later came the loud electric buzz from the amplifier followed by an almighty howl. It was the loudest scream I'd ever heard and was followed by banging and thuds. I ran upstairs, calling his name. He screamed again and by the time I reached him, he was slumped on the floor outside the radio room. I called his name and there was no response, I turned him around and saw that he was gurgling, his face was dark and I could smell burning flesh. I called for help then I went back to attend to Salim. I tried CPR and mouth-to-mouth, I inhaled the fumes of burning human flesh and when I looked at his eyes, they appeared glazed.... I knew he was leaving us.

I screamed his name, but there was no response—just a faint wheezing as he exhaled his last breath. He died in my arms as I hugged and kissed him and cried. I lost my brother and dear friend.

The nightmare continued that night. I was taken to a police station to give my witness statement. I did nothing wrong so I was not afraid but I was weak from the trauma. I was in shock. The police mechanically took my statement and released me, they explained I was not to blame: Salim had taken off his shoes prior to his demise and was walking barefoot on tiles, the shock from the amplifier was powerful and went through his body causing his death.

Over the next few days, I was in shock and could barely sleep, eat or function. I went to visit Salim's parents and broke down on seeing them crying for their lost son. I was in a lot of pain inside, part of me died that day....

Out of necessity, I shared a bedroom with my sister Nathaly and it was a great comfort. I had become scared of the dark and could not sleep even if the lights were on. One night, just as I drifted into a light sleep, I woke up and saw Salim's face in the mirror. Although there was no malice and he was smiling, I was still startled. My dear sister, my shining star, calmed me down by diverting my attention to a game of cards. She did the right thing, because after a few hands, I was able to sleep. Distracting me helped me that night, but the core issue remained. I needed help badly.

I eventually returned to London and reunited with Claudine. I had so many questions and was desperate for answers but I had personal issues to deal with. I had a taste of fear and death to a degree I had never experienced before. It took me a long time to come to terms with my new reality. I carried a deep scar and I found myself overwhelmed on many occasions. I suffered anxiety attacks, fear and cried alone. I was devastated by how he died and the experience haunted me. Claudine was my support and on many occasions my punching bag when fear gave way to anger.

I could no longer sleep and had become scared of the dark. I felt guilty and responsible because I was unable to save my friend's life. Despite all the assurances I had received from technicians and electrical engineers that Salim would never have survived the electrocution, the power amplifier was 3000 watts, I could not shake off the guilt. This feeling intensified and I saw myself as a failure and became crippled emotionally. I became more reserved and less interactive, I lost interest and motivation, so I stopped attending classes. I found myself staying up at night, smoking and drinking. Claudine tried to break some of these cycles. If I could think of one way to describe the state that I was in, I would say that I was in limbo. Had I not chosen to leave the radio room and go downstairs to play the piano, we would probably both have been dead. What prompted me to leave?

I came face-to-face with death, I literally tasted death when I inhaled the fumes from burning flesh. Death is overpowering—ruthless and indiscriminate. Questions swirled in my mind, why was I spared? Why couldn't I save him? Why did I feel that something sad was to happen in Lebanon prior to my departure from London and my feelings came true with the sad demise of a friend?

I sought help from a therapist, but it was one dimensional and it was not going anywhere so I stopped seeing her and just drifted on....

One day at a social gathering I listened to a group conversation about death and someone in the crowd was adamant that death is not the end and that there is life after it. He recounted a meeting with a spiritualist medium who had given him incredible evidence to that effect. I was intrigued and privately asked him to explain more. He summed it up by giving me the card of a spiritualist medium in London. He told me to call him and that he could explain it far better.

I had no idea what a spiritualist medium was. Back then there was no Internet to provide instant answers. I was intrigued, so I organized a meeting with the medium. I wanted to hear from my lost friend, I was desperate to find out anything about him because my memory of his passing was brutal and I wanted the assurance that he was in better form on the other side. I was also intrigued by what is on the other side of life. On the day of the sitting, I was with Claudine and my two sisters-in-law, we were all quite excited. The medium turned up, he looked like an ordinary man on the larger side and proceeded to give us readings.

I was the last to receive my reading and he communicated some messages from my lost friend and he also told me that I had the gift of healing. I was trying to digest what I was being told, I had no idea what a healer was and nor was I really interested. He explained that a healer is someone who can help other people get well and to me it sounded impossible because I believed that only Jesus Christ was a healer. After years of searching for answers, I wanted him to inform me all about the paranormal and to teach me. I was fascinated, I wanted to do extraordinary things.

I asked him if he could teach me to do what he did. He agreed to develop me for a fee. Someone enquired how long the process would take for me to become 'developed' and he said three months. A week later my journey into spiritual development began under his guidance.

He taught me about Chakras or channels that are present in all of us and how to open and close them. He taught me how to meditate and to visualise coloured lights. Then we went deeper and he took me on guided meditations where he introduced me to my spirit guides and taught me how to communicate with them. Once a week, he came over and spent an hour taking me through my development class. I was fascinated with the process, I was introduced to new aspects of the paranormal. I was not using my true gifts back then, nor was my development in line to any part of what I practice now. I believe that the process was mainly suggestive and totally wrong. I had no way of knowing what was real and what wasn't. Nonetheless, I was happy to finally be involved in the paranormal. It's what I'd always yearned for.

A year later, while having coffee with a friend, she asked why I was still in development when it should have taken three months. I was too fascinated with my development process and blinded by what I thought were psychic abilities and the paranormal to really care about the lingering process. The discrepancy was obvious to an outsider, especially one who made the medium uncomfortable. When she first met him, she told me that she didn't like him. I was cross with her, thinking she was being judgmental without even knowing him. She asked him a few questions. She wasn't rude, but still, he was angry.

In private, my friend insisted that something was not right and I should question my mentor, she told me she trusted her gut instinct and I listened to her. The next day I asked the medium why the sessions dragged on for over a year. He waffled about me being at a different level of development from when I initially started. He said that it was imperative that I should continue my development, otherwise things may take a turn for the bad. The more he spoke, the less I believed him. I told him I wanted to stop my training and thanked him. I tried to politely end the conversation but he stated he was a sick man and that my development was not complete and it would be dangerous for me to stop. I felt he was trying to gain my sympathy and issuing subtle threats to scare me. It was obvious I was being used and manipulated. I made the right decision terminating our agreement.

Before confronting the medium, I felt that the development process was becoming repetitive and in hindsight, I now believe that it was all wrong, and he was improvising as he went. Nearly all of it was suggestion-based meaning that I was being told certain things and reacting to them accordingly. So for instance, during meditation where I was supposed to 'meet' my guides, he would say, you will now meet a Chinese man ... and I would see a Chinese man. Now I know just how naïve I was to the fact that I was being manipulated for financial gain.

The only good thing I took away from that experience was the confirmation that I am a healer. I also learnt to keep my feet on the ground and to be sensible. Unfortunately, there are many con artists who prey on the vulnerable when it comes to the paranormal. So many desperate individuals, especially the bereaved, put their trust and hopes in so-called mediums who take advantage of them and exploit them while delivering nothing of substance and scoop their victims' money in return.

Bad psychics and mediums tarnish the reputation of the truly gifted. People judge mediums and psychics as a collective and not on an individual basis. There are good and bad people from all walks of life. There are medical doctors who kill but that does not make all doctors killers. Con artists are drawn to the paranormal as means to financial or material gain because it is not a tangible product that they try to sell. It is easy for them to deny, lie and twist the facts as needed.

With my newly-acquired knowledge, I explored new frontiers. I gave readings to friends and their friends. I offered healing and tried to go into 'trances' for channelling. I had no experience, no guidance and had no idea what I was doing. I picked up a few pointers from the medium who had helped me develop, but I was doing it all wrong. Yet I could not stop myself because it was getting me attention and I started to believe that I was great! I was establishing contact with characters who I believed were my guides as introduced by the medium. I found myself openly debating and discussing the subject of the paranormal on many occasions as if I was a leading authority; goodness knows the state of mind that I was in. I shudder now when I recall some of my follies and I consider myself lucky for dicing with danger and being spared. Now that I know what's out there, in the form of dark entities, demons, etc. I thank my lucky stars every day.

Natural law dictates that a lesson must be learnt in everything in life and I was destined to be taught a valuable lesson that would stay with me for years. I am not sure if what was to come was intended as 'punishment' for my insolence or if it was meant to shake my foundations, perhaps it was meant as a bit of both or even a warning of things to come ... who knows. It did have the desired effect and it stopped me.

I must explain that while being 'developed' by the medium, he convinced me that there are no evil spirits but rather 'mischievous' spirits who can be put right with a 'telling off'. I found myself believing what he said and became convinced that this was indeed true. Amazingly, I did not pause to question the validity of such a presumption, even when it contravened with my Christian background and the teachings in the Holy Bible where it clearly describes all things evil and the enemies of God. Even today I meet spiritualists who believe in that same concept. Some go as far as to not believe in the existence of the devil or his agents. This troubles me deeply because the same individuals also believe that the spirit world is a mirror of our own world here on Earth. If this is true, then I wonder how the various abominations who are responsible for so much cruelty, pain and genocides are mirrored on the other side. Given the proportion of evil involved here on earth, I do not believe that such atrocities were committed or influenced merely by 'mischievous spirits'

Evil of this is magnitude is orchestrated by a force that is far more vile and sophisticated than we can possibly comprehend. The greater evil is for us to deny its existence and paint over it with feeble theories and excuses.

After years of service as a healer and an exorcist, I know that evil is real and powerful, it never ends well for those who underestimate it..

The days went by and I was becoming more engrossed in my newly discovered pastime. I became obsessed and was keen to give a reading to people or to supposedly go into a trance for my guides to come through with their enlightenment. The bottom line is that I had no idea what I was doing, it was totally wrong and downright shambolic in fact. Worst of all, it was feeding into my pride and ego and the purpose being served was selfish with total disregard to natural law and procedure. I was not trying to defraud or to hurt others, I was foolish and lacked experience, I had no idea what I was doing.

Eventually it all came to an end and I was served one of the biggest lessons in life.

One night, I had a terrifying dream. I was resisting against two individuals and trying to stop them from entering my apartment through a window. I remember the room in my dream being dark and the individuals looking menacing. They were grinning at me as if to say "You stand no chance!" Eventually, they managed to get in and a jolt woke me. It was an unpleasant experience and I knew that something was wrong but I just carried on with my day. Over the next few days, I tired quickly, I didn't want to leave the apartment. I slept late at night and not long enough. I disliked daytime, the light disturbed me and I preferred to be left alone. Communicating with my girlfriend became an unpleasant chore. I felt disturbed by her presence and did not want her around. She knew something was wrong and raised concern but I shut her out. I distinctly remember craving alcohol and drank whiskey all the time (I rarely drank whiskey before as the taste did not appeal to me). I'd drink a whole bottle in a few hours and yet I was never drunk. I was on edge and ready to snap for no reason, I felt angry all the time. I remember having to go to the bank to attend to an important matter. My bank was no more than 100 meters away and I struggled to walk there. Every step I took was an effort and when I finally got there, the cashier who had become a friend was concerned, she told me that I did not look well. I don't remember what excuse I gave her but I just wanted to go home. I did not want the daylight or to engage with others. I wanted to be alone ... and drink. My face became quite gaunt and my eyes looked glazed and tired. When I looked in the mirror while shaving, I felt disoriented and confused. Gone was the smile and warmth, I lost all motivation and succumbed to the fatigue that rendered me incapable of even the most basic function.

Soon I was in front of the television most of the time, curtains drawn and drink in hand. I had no enthusiasm to do anything else. When my girlfriend showed up, it was a case of tolerating her presence for as long as I could in the hope that she would leave me alone. But she was concerned, scared for me, in fact. Eventually the unavoidable happened and we had a massive row after she confronted me about my drinking and lethargy. She kept repeating that something was wrong and I tried to dismiss her but she was quite insistent. I am not a violent person by nature and I dislike confrontation. Yet, I assaulted my girlfriend, I punched her hard on her side and she fell backwards. She was gasping for air, coughing and wheezing, her face in absolute shock. I pulled back, panicking, possibly more shocked than she, who was now doubled up on the floor, crying and screaming at me. I was in a haze, I had no idea what had happened but I had assaulted the person I loved the most for no reason. I went from feeling powerful to feeling absolutely helpless.

"I am going to call the police," she screamed at me. "How dare you? How dare you!"

I tried to calm her but she refused to listen. She started dialling and I took the phone. I begged her not to. I told her what was happening and everything that was going on. I told her about my dream and how things started to go wrong that day. I summarised by asking her to find a way to help me.

"I need your help, please. I am sorry about what happened, but you know that this is not me. Please listen to me, something is wrong...."

She trusted me against all odds and decided to give me a chance. We worked together to find an answer as to what was going on and a solution to my behaviour which continued to get worse. We were eventually led to a spiritualist church in Stockwell, South London. We organized a meeting with a healer recommended by the church. By then, my condition had deteriorated so much, I could not fathom much of what was happening around me. I was having nightmares and they were becoming more vivid and sickening. My relationship with my girlfriend was also in constant decline but she held on.

We arrived at the church and were led to a room where the medium and his helper looked at me and whispered to each other. He told me that there was 'something' with me and that he'd try to help me. My girlfriend begged him to do something, I did not react. If anything, I wanted to leave. The medium stood behind me and placed both hands on my shoulder, I was not uncomfortable and apprehensive and did not know what to expect. He then pressed a bit more firmly on my shoulders and his breathing was louder and slower. This went on for some time before he started saying things that I could not understand. I don't know if he was even speaking in English, I was not focusing, I felt a different sensation from the one I walked in with. Something was changing within me and then the medium uttered an incomprehensible word and shook me lightly. His assistant examined me, said it was nearly over and reassured me. It was kind of her to do so but I was already starting to feel better, I was feeling myself again, even as I gazed around the room. I saw things with clarity. The heaviness had gone, something had changed without doubt. The medium was leaning at a table and his face was in the palm of his hands and quite red. He looked to be in discomfort but his assistant assured me he was fine. I didn't know he was an empath and a healer and must have taken the energies into him to rid me of them. I didn't know it at the time, but this would be my path. I would become the empath and the healer.

Suddenly, I started to cry, I tried to stop myself but I couldn't. My crying turned into deep sobs. I felt violated and bullied and I hated it, I was also disgusted with myself at having hit my girlfriend, causing her so much pain and fear. I resented the paranormal and I wished I was someone else. Deep down, I knew I was to blame. I felt a great shame. The healer and his assistant calmed me down, they were gentle, telling me everything would be okay. I glimpsed my girlfriend in tears.

"It's okay Garo.... It's over...."

He put his arm across my shoulder and that gave me a lot of reassurance and strength. The healer ended the session and explained that I was being controlled by two unpleasant entities who had attached themselves to me. He assured my girlfriend that they were gone and explained that I was not myself.... He did not need to go into detail, she understood, and we cried some more. They offered me water and I drank, I was thirsty.

"How do you feel now?" the healer asked. I think he could see a difference and was pleased.

"Hungry ... I feel hungry!"

They laughed and the medium suggested to my girlfriend that we go for a bite to eat and rest. He went on to explain things to her but I was not in a position to focus on what was being said. I was slowly coming to terms with everything that just took place and trying to recover.

On our way home, we stopped and grabbed a takeaway. I was weak but after some food, my strength returned. I was myself again and my girlfriend was the happiest person in the world. We went home and settled down and watched television, then we went to bed. I had a good deep sleep, undisturbed; no nightmares and no whispers.

I did not touch alcohol for a long time after that experience. The sight of whiskey revolted me.

My girlfriend who is now my wife, endured quite a lot from that horrible experience but she persevered and that is a trust I learnt to cherish.

My experience of becoming influenced or taken over by an entity or energy was to have a grave impression on me later in life. I suffered as my patients did and maybe it was so I could truly understand them. Above all, I learnt that the paranormal is not for fun nor is it a game, it is to be respected at all times. What started off as a nightmare, turned out to be more profound and terrifying. I had become host to two very mean and dangerous entities who influenced my behaviour and my thinking. I spiralled out of control and heaven knows where I might have ended.

It was also my first brush with the 'enemy'—dark entities intent on making our lives miserable to break us and destroy all that we treasure and believe in. I learnt a valuable lesson that is with me even today and I make sure never to take my position for granted. I always pray for protection from the dark side but I also pray that I am guided so that I never knowingly or unknowingly abuse my gift. In hindsight, I consider myself lucky to have been spared an even worse ordeal. I know now that it could have been far worse and only a miracle saved me.

THE TURBULENT YEARS

Almost everyone does things they regret. In my case, unfortunately, I heeded advice from friends and family, especially my girlfriend and went from bad to worse and God only knows how I managed to make it out alive after so many experiences.

My poison has always been seeking attention and approval. I always felt I needed to do anything and everything to belong in groups or circles of friends. I befriended gamblers, became a gambler and then a gambling addict. I mixed with people who took drugs and I also learnt bad habits from them but I was lucky not to have ventured too deep. As fate would have it, I ended up befriending a female classmate at college who turned out to be from a family of renowned East London gangsters. I had no idea who she was or who her parents were, we enjoyed an innocent friendship and at times I helped her with her college work. She invited me to the opening of her club in London's Soho where I mingled with top London gangsters and thugs. They were nice, but I could tell that there was more to the characters who I was mixing with, they were tough and rough. They spoke in heavy cockney accents, smoked and when they shook my hand, most had a firm grip. It was a surreal experience and I learnt a lot from it, mostly to respect everyone, regardless of their backgrounds, even those who have chosen the dark side.

Then I went into the music business against my father's wishes who insisted that I should keep music as a hobby. I had a passion for Chillout type of music and wanted to produce my own music and maybe even record a music album. My father was concerned that only a lucky few succeed in the music business and he was right; there are thousands of talented musicians out there seeking recognition, what makes me any different? I started buying synthesisers and basic studio equipment to have fun as a hobby and that is when a friend from college convinced me to buy more equipment and turn a room in the house into a recording studio. I spent a good amount of money and converted the garage into a recording studio. I bought the latest equipment, mixing desk and effects so I could record my music and also rent out the studio to others for income. I did not think at the time that this would be a catastrophic decision. First, I had no control over who hired the studio and the characters that showed up some good, many bad and some who were downright evil. I was quite naïve and was chasing a dream, but I was being scammed most of the time. Before I knew it, the person who I trusted as my friend from college, started inviting all sorts of characters to the studio. I was surrounded by opportunists whose ambitions were far from being aligned to my own dreams. I believed their stories and empty promises, I felt sorry for them because they succeeded in making me feel guilty that I could afford many things when they could not. I was gullible and was manipulated to even feel responsible for them.

All it took was for someone to shed a few tears and I would reach into my pocket to help them. Unfortunately, I ignored Claudine's advice and concerns and shut her out of my life so I could be with my new friends. I made an absurd choice and paid for it dearly. I still don't understand why I ignored the advice given to me by someone who loved me unconditionally. Maybe I had to learn from my experience. By the time I realised that things were going badly, it was too late, I had invested a lot of money into the recording studio and backing out was no longer an option; I wanted to recoup my losses—an even worse mistake.

The atmosphere at the studio was becoming darker. I realised some people I associated with had criminal pasts, one had even stabbed his girlfriend, others had served time in prison. I was led to believe that we'd produce hit singles and make a lot of money. For me, it was not only about making money as much as I wanted to impress my father and build a successful company as he did, so I went with my new friends' proposals and plans. Yet deep down I felt that something was not right and whenever I had a feeling that I was being lied to and being manipulated, I'd be shut down and accused of being weak and lacking trust. They would gang up on me, bully and scare me. I put up some resistance but they were professional con artists who manipulated me and knew my weak points. I surrendered the funds they asked for—all in the name of them producing a 'hit' record was never made. Sadly, I also saw the prospect of realizing my own dream and recording my own music album slow fade away. Towards the end, they had taken over the recording studio, ushering in more thugs and crooks and it became a playground for all sorts of unsavoury individuals. The leader of the pack who I believed to be a friend turned out to be the worst one. Not only was the studio a means for him to extract cash from me, but he also was using it to lure impressionable and hopeful female artists to have his way with them sexually.

Claudine was devastated. She saw me sink to new lows and fought with me to regain myself. She threatened to inform my father and I literally threw her out of the house. If it was any other person, they would have given up on me but Claudine persisted and kept her faith in me. I am grateful that I did not lose her along with everything I lost at that time.

With the help of my good friends I eventually got rid of all the nasty elements in my life. I was weak and drained but above all I was penniless. I remember walking the streets of London like a zombie trying to make sense of all that I was going through. The pain was overwhelming and as I walked I found myself fidgeting with something sharp in my pocket and then I felt great relief as I pushed my finger against it and started cutting myself. As blood trickled from my hand, I felt comfort and punishment. It was good to hurt myself, to bleed ... I hated myself. I had no one to blame but myself and I felt that I deserved it.

I wandered through the streets, bleeding, crying and hungry. My life was in ruins. I was dying inside. I stopped in front of a burger bar and smelled burgers and onions. I craved a burger but when I reached into my pocket, I only found a few coins, not enough to buy a burger. I slumped on the pavement and cried. I was riddled with shame and guilt, I was the loneliest person in the world.

I lost so much money and I had so many debts, how could I ask my father for help? I ignored his advice and here I was in a desperate situation. I was losing my sanity and my identity. I was ill, mentally and emotionally. Somehow I kept my belief in the greater good. I never blamed God for my failing. I allowed myself to end up in this predicament.

I ended up selling my home and the studio equipment while recording my own music album. I was desperate to at least record my own music. I recorded a demo album in the end. Unfortunately, I did lose more than material possessions, I lost Claudine's trust. She never made me feel bad about what had happened and I never let her know just how bad things were. Things got even worse when my friend Bruce, a music producer at the studio, overdosed and died. His passing was so unexpected and shocking, it knocked me further into the abyss.

I consequently took refuge in drinking and recreational drugs. I knew what I was doing was wrong but I didn't care. I never felt I belonged in most social circles and the few friends I had left were decreasing in numbers, it was easier to numb myself through life than deal with things. I was absolutely disgusted with myself, I had no confidence and I saw myself as a failure. This wasn't how I was raised, but I felt powerless to change.

Since I had no money and my days in London served no specific purpose, my father suggested that I move back to Lebanon. I did not want to lose Claudine and moving would've resulted in just that. My parents sold their lavish apartment in London and Claudine and I rented a basement studio in Kilburn. It was on the rough side and the flat was shabby and suffered from serious damp issues. It was so bad, mushrooms grew in the ceiling. We stayed there for as long as we could before I finally left to go back to Lebanon. However, we did make the most of our stay in that flat. We especially enjoyed the company of our friends and our get togethers.

The good times were few and far between. The reality was that I had lost my money to the scammers and would probably have to return to Lebanon. The months went by and like vapour, the days vanished; it was all a haze. I was tense and sad and my relationship with Claudine became volatile as a result of my excess drinking. There were times we could not stand each other and so we separated and I returned to my parents in Lebanon. I wanted to be near them as I was still reeling from my wounds. They had no idea how bad my situation was and I did not tell them. During my stay in Lebanon, I was no longer involved in anything of interest at a personal level, I gave up writing, reading or pursuing any interest in the paranormal. My father helped me with some capital to try and get me going in business again and I invested in the stock market. After several blows and losses, I started trying to chase my losses but ended up losing more. I started losing my sanity. At my lowest in Lebanon, and with everything compounded, I sat staring into an empty space in my home with a fully loaded pistol on the coffee table. I picked it up and contemplated ending my life, ending the pain and everything that came with it, the shame and guilt. I failed in everything, including the love of my life, Claudine. I chambered a round and raised the gun to my head, my finger on the trigger and ready to pull. My hand shook, I hesitated, something made me stop. I cried.... I could not shoot myself. I lowered the gun and placed it on the table, while fighting hard against the demons in my head who mocked me for failing to pull the trigger. It took a few days for me to get over this incident, I pretended that I was unwell so that I could be alone.

Many people are judgmental towards those who commit suicide. They call them names and label them as selfish or cowards. I never do. I came close to ending my life, I had a taste of hell and the level of pain that is sufficient to numb one's instinct and turn a person on themselves, against their nature of self-preservation. This pain is indescribable.... It's not an act of selfishness, it's hell....

I did not let my parents know how bad things were, I did not want to break their hearts. It was impossible to hide things from them and I am sure they felt something was wrong. My father saw that I was unwell and asked me to sell up all stocks and shares, even with losses. He made me promise not to ever invest in them again, a promise that I have kept. With the cash from selling the stocks and shares, my father recommended that I buy a flat to let in London. I felt relieved in a sense that I had put the horrible chapter of stocks and shares behind me but I was still unhappy, my life was empty without Claudine. Then one day, she called and she missed me and I returned to London to be with her again. We stayed in the flat that my father asked me to buy.

I was adamant on salvaging our relationship and whatever was left of it but it was no easy task. I had to win her trust again and after all that she had gone through being with me, I doubted that I would succeed but I could not imagine my life without her and I had to try. I took a ring with me and I promised her that I'd never leave her again for anything and asked her hand in marriage.

Although I loved her dearly, I could not truly love her unless I made peace with myself first. Claudine suggested I visit a therapist to help me deal with everything that I was carrying and so she introduced me to Paula, a non-conventional psychotherapist who did not operate from a clinic but rather the front room of her cosy apartment near Westbourne Grove, London. I had no idea what to expect and I was sceptical at first, especially when I learnt from my wife that Paula was also a spiritualist. I became negative about meeting her. My previous experience with a so-called spiritualist who turned out to be driven by financial gain had put me off spiritualists.

I felt strange on my first visit, I was confused, I wasn't sure if I really wanted to be there and if I could even trust her. I did not immediately open up to her and I did test her by being intentionally awkward. She was genuine and wanted to help. Paula made me promise I'd stop using recreational drugs immediately. I promised not to indulge ever again and have kept my promise for more than fifteen years. Drugs have devastating side-effects. My life significantly improved as soon as I stopped using and I quickly regained my coherence and clarity.

Paula's approach was delicate, she let me talk and she listened intently. At first, I saw little point in our weekly meetings and felt therapy was just chit chat over a cup of coffee. Gradually we started addressing deeper issues and the more issues that we dealt with, the more surfaced. We both connected, emotionally, mentally and spiritually and I liked the fact that she never tried to influence me in any way. Further on, during our work together, sometimes Paula hinted that I am gifted but she told me that I also had a choice, free will, and that I am entitled to make my own life choices. She helped me turn past events around, to relive many of the dark memories to be able to deal with them and to let go. We shed many tears together. I shared everything with her, I opened up about my past, my failings, the bullying and abuse that I suffered. It was a struggle to discuss some subjects that I had purposely moved away from, but to overcome the past, I had to deal with them. I trusted her, she was genuinely trying to help me and I felt that she cared at a personal level. That she remembered everything I shared proved to me that she genuinely cared.

One of the hardest subjects was dealing with the horrific memory of Salim's death by electrocution. This was a complex issue and I hurt at many levels because he died in my arms. I could not share this experience with anyone for a long time but on a quiet afternoon and over a steaming cup of coffee, I shared the events from that dreadful day. It was hard at first but she helped me take things a step at a time and slowly guided me through a mire of suppressed emotions. Her unique, gentle and empathic approach was indeed liberating. Halfway through the process, I realized she sometimes filled in the blanks whenever I was quiet or struggling for words. It was as if she was with me during the tragedy. How could she know certain facts without me revealing them? She was psychic and her gift allowed her to tap into this past event at a deep level so we took the journey together. This was a clue as to how gifted she was and even more remarkable was how she helped me overcome my feelings of guilt and the shock of witnessing the death of a dear friend I never truly mourned his death as the shock was so immense. My system simply rejected his memory.

This was a large stumbling block in my life which I could never have shifted without divine intervention. It took a few sessions to work through it but I got there in the end. After clearing the memory of that tragic event, I felt liberated and grateful so I went back to Paula a week later to share with her. She was delighted to see me improve and took the opportunity to subtly reveal the value of healing and how precious a gift it is.

"All the painful experiences that you have gone through in your life were important for your development. The knowledge that you acquired will go towards helping others."

I could not fully relate to what she was saying but there was no denying that I was finally at peace regarding the death of my friend. I no longer felt guilty, on the contrary, I knew I'd done my best to save him. I accepted that there was nothing anyone could have done to save his life.

"The gift of healing is the gift of life; it is the closest to Christ that we will ever get. Healing is a service like no other Garo."

I left with so many thoughts swirling around in my head. I understood the significance of what she told me but I could not see myself as a healer, far from it. Primarily, I was desperate to get my own life sorted out, my finances, business, etc. But I could not ignore the fact that I was helped myself and how could I sit idle, knowing that I could be of benefit to some desperate soul?

Over the next few days, I thought more on the subject and discussed it with my wife who helped me come to terms with it even more.

"If this is indeed a gift, then it would be wrong to ignore it and not to accept it." She went on. "You look disturbed, why?"

"I never imagined that I would be doing this sort of thing.... Never saw myself as a healer."

"You will be helping others Garo.... Such a privileged position to be in."

I didn't realize my core issue was that I was afraid of failure and of letting people down. I did not have confidence in myself and my faith was shaky. I was also wary of the responsibility associated with healing and all that is associated with it. I went back to Paula after reflecting on the subject. I was open about my feelings and she completely understood and was supportive.

"I think you may be reading too much into things, Garo. Should you decide to offer healing, you will be inspired about what to do. How about if you were to see one or two people to see how you feel and take things from there?"

"There is no harm in trying, I guess."

My wife's words echoed in my head. "You will be helping others Garo. Such a privileged position to be in."

Paula recommended me to others and after seeing a few people and receiving good feedback, more people came. These were 'mild' cases compared to the issues I deal with today—minor physical ailments such as shoulder pain, muscle spasms, acid reflux. They all reported improvements.

It felt good to be doing something positive and more people were referred to me. I was seeing patients in my apartment and because I had no assistant, I stressed to them to bring a trusted party along. I met some nice and interesting people at the time and it boosted my confidence because many people who I saw, may not have been believers in healing. They did, however, appreciate the gesture and the fact that someone was willing to give their time in the hope that they are improved.

Eventually, I started receiving patients with attachments or influenced by dark energies so my wife and I decided that I should no longer see people at home. Paula promised to help me find premises to continue my practice. I took a break, during which I went on long walks at the Heath in Hampstead, a beautiful natural forest in London. There, I enjoyed Mother Nature's tranquillity and in private pray for inspiration. I passed the time but eventually became restless and bored because I felt that I was just wasting away. I complained to my wife and she told me to enjoy the 'time off' while it lasted and she was right. Later, I was granted access and full use of the premises at a Spiritualist church and with the aid of volunteers, our healing service, Light of Light was born. The term 'Light of Light' is used in Arabic prayers in reference to Jesus Christ, being the light that is born of light.

MY GRANDFATHER
AND HIS FRIEND

In my early days when I shared messages from loved ones on the other side and pass them to different people, I enjoyed every minute especially when messages came for individuals who never expected to receive any in the first place. Sometimes, I gave sittings to friends and family members and these were always difficult and awkward because of the element of familiarity, nonetheless, they would still receive messages, things that I could not have possibly known.

It was summer and I was with my family sitting at a table near the sea shore having enjoyed a hearty lunch prepared by now my now-late grandmother. Eventually, everyone left, and I was on my own with my grandparents. My grandfather was smoking one of his local branded cigarettes while sipping on his black coffee. He was generally a quiet man, but he was a character and quite eccentric. He did not pay any attention to my grandmother when she quietly asked me to explain about the readings that I had been giving to others and I explained as discreetly as I could, given the fact that my grandfather was present. Before I knew it, he surprised me when he turned and asked me for a reading!

"How about you tell me things as well?"

Given the fact that my grandfather was very popular as a prankster and enjoyed a good laugh, I was unsure if his request was genuine so I turned to my grandmother and she nodded in approval.

I tuned in and the first thing that I picked up was an image of a humble restaurant on a pier extending over the sea front. It was empty save for one man, of slightly bigger build sitting with a cigarette in hand and a backgammon game on the table on his side. I described the scene to my grandfather and he did not respond. I then received the name 'George' which I passed on and again, there was no acknowledgement so I felt awkward.

"He says that he is your friend, you used to meet at that place very often to play backgammon."

No reaction.

There was persistence from the man in my vision and he was insisting on getting through to my grandfather.

"Grandfather, do you know who I am talking about?"

My grandmother sensed my frustration, stepped in and gave him a nudge.

"What is wrong with you?" she asked my grandfather. "It's George! Why are you being so awkward? You know who he is."

"What does he want?" my grandfather almost shouted "What the hell does he want from me?"

My grandmother tried to quiet him, but his eyes were bulging with anger. I felt very nervous about the situation that we were in. My grandfather was usually a very happy and comical person and there he was transformed with anger.

"Grandfather, I believe he just wants to say hello."

"To hell with him ... and his hello." He went on a rant and it ended with incoherent babble that I could not really understand. My grandmother started arguing with him and demanded an explanation for his behaviour. The exchange got heated and he even slammed the desk and his playing cards jumped in the air. Very dramatic to say the least but I could also tell that he was genuinely upset about something. I was confused and nervous. I wished I hadn't done the reading. I had no idea how to bring it to an end, so I remained silent.

When he calmed down a bit, my grandmother asked him again what was wrong and after some silence, he finally blurted out, "The bastard owes me money! I loaned him and then he died without paying me...."

"Ask him to pay you when you finally join him!" my grandmother replied shaking her head in disbelief.

Given the fact that the situation had progressed further into the surreal, I elected to stay quiet and not to convey any more messages back and forth. I distinctly remember my grandmother looking at me then at my grandfather and then back at me and following with a hearty laugh....

It so happened that on that summer holiday I also performed one of my earliest healings to a distant older family member who was unable to walk and had limited with the use of his arms and hands. My grandmother had told me about the man, describing him as nice and in a lot of discomfort. She asked if there was anything that I could do and I immediately said yes. I was sixteen back then and I lacked the experience that I have now, but my intentions were genuine. My grandmother took me to see this man and I didn't not quite understand the big deal being made about my visit. They were devout Christians and they welcomed me very warmly into their home. I entered the house and sat in the living room with all gathered for a general chat but then I looked at the gentleman and asked where was it was possible for me to pray for him.

We moved to the dining room where he sat on a chair and I stood behind him. I placed my hands on his shoulders and prayed. I do not recall much other than that it was a short visit. I later heard that after that session, the man was able to walk again and regained the use of his hands and arms. He spoke of a miracle and attributed his recovery to my visit; it was overwhelming, and I did not quite comprehend the entire experience. I was baffled as to how come he recovered so quickly. I saw no reason why he improved the way he did simply because I laid my hands on him for a short while.

I desperately needed answers, so I asked my grandmother to tell me what happened. She said I stood motionless behind the man for a very long time, I did not speak, and my eyes were shut for the most part. When it was over, we were offered coffees and some sweets, and we made our way back home. It was all blurry to me and I remember feeling at the time that nothing much really happened. I thought that we had briefly visited, and it was over very quickly. Little did I know the impact that visit would have over this man and in years to come I learnt that he became mobile again and was able to resume his day to day life without any difficulties. I was delighted to learn this as I certainly did not expect it. He went on to describe his experience to his friends and his family. Despite this phenomenal result, I still shunned healing and thought of it as far less significant than other 'super powers' to which I aspired. Little did I know how lucky I am to be chosen to serve, there is no greater privilege in the world. I was very immature at the time.

RUSSIA – EYE TREATMENT

During my treatment in Russia the true extent of my gift was revealed to me through an unworldly experience. The last thing I expected during my eye treatment was a turn of events and for my life to change so dramatically. It didn't matter where I being treated, but the fact that I was receiving a specialist type of treatment to my eyes may have been a contributing factor.

At the age of forty, I went to Moscow to investigate treatment for my strabismus. My family doctor accompanied me because he spoke the language.

The treatment involved retraining the brain, and therefore is usually more successful in paediatric patients. I was carefully evaluated and a custom intensive program was devised for me. They started the treatment using different visual techniques and exercises with the aid of sophisticated equipment I was not familiar with. Since I suffer with double vision in both eyes, their goal was to re-train my brain to stop seeing the extra shadow images and thus eliminate the double vision. At first, it was an impossible feat, but they asked me to persevere in the hope of some positive results.

The exercises involved machines that generated mental and visual challenges, to help train the brain into correcting the vision. This was their preferred approach over surgery which they believed would be a waste of time. After a full day of treatment, I would go back to my hotel and collapse in bed from extreme fatigue and the next day, the process would be repeated. The treatment was becoming harder every day because of time constraints, they tried to squeeze in as much as possible. I was warned about this but I just wanted to get on with it and finish the program.

One day, I was left alone in the slightly darkened treatment room behind one of the machines. I was focusing on trying to pair and unite images by aligning them using my eyes and my hand using a computer mouse. I was wearing special goggles that made objects on the screen appear almost three dimensional. I needed a break, so I took off the goggles. I wasn't tired, I was feeling pleasant and peaceful, staring at nothing in particular and then I felt myself drift away. It was similar to a daydream but also different because of the sensations that overcame me. I felt a calming sensation envelop me and part of me felt as if I was no longer in the room. The feeling was indescribable, I felt a peace that I had never felt before, I was surrounded by an incredible feeling of warmth.

I saw in my mind's eye the silhouette of a hooded person ahead and I heard a voice in my head.

"We are expanding your mind to prepare you."

The voice was neither male or female, it wasn't even a voice as we know it.... It was more of a combination of an audible sound and a feeling.

There were no distinct features to the figure that I saw. There was no way for me to determine its sex. I was not scared, and I did not feel threatened in any way.

When the communication ceased I was still in a haze, trying to take it all in. Then I felt a presence behind me and I immediately sensed it was my late grandfather. He was in his black suit and carrying his favourite Holy Bible. I felt him standing close behind me and had I opened my eyes and turned, I am certain that I would have seen him. With my eyes still closed, I saw his image. I sensed him, and I heard his beautiful soft voice and almost felt his hand pat my shoulder.

"Beautiful, Garo ... this is so beautiful ..." He was congratulating me and I had no idea on what but I felt that it was something special. The sensation and the daydream ended and I was back to myself, in the room and in front of the machines. I did not want that feeling to go, it was so beautiful, the contrast was distinct. More so, I did not want the communication with my grandfather to end, his presence was calming and assuring and I loved him dearly and to feel him right next to me and after so many years touched me deeply. I was in tears, I was overcome with emotion. I missed him so much and I still do. But I know in my heart that he is in a better place among his loved ones and family who he was deprived of being a sole survivor in his family of the Armenian Genocide.

I took a break and went outside to digest what had just happened. I was hoping to have some time alone because I was emotional, but I bumped into my doctor. He was the last person I wanted to see, I didn't want him to think that there was something wrong with me as a result of the exercises. He updated me on our progress but it was hard for me to follow conversations or to focus on what he was saying. I just nodded. He asked if I was okay and commented that I looked tired and maybe we should stop for the day. I welcome the proposition and we made it back to the hotel. The clinic asked me to rest my eyes in preparation for treatment the following day; no television, computers or Internet. I didn't need convincing, all I wanted to do was to sleep. I didn't want to lose the feeling of that special experience, I wanted to preserve the sensation for as long as I could.

That night was difficult, I struggled to sleep. So many thoughts rushed through my head at once it was overwhelming. My perception was altered somehow. I couldn't focus and I was anxious so I calmed myself and prayed. It helped but I was still feeling hyper so I listened to music but that too proved to be hard. Thousands of thoughts were going through my mind at once, and I struggled to control them. At one point, they appeared to become independent of me and were overwhelming me. I paced, I ate and then I turned my attention to the television but I remembered I had to give my eyes some rest before the next day's intensive therapy. I switched it off and eventually slept.

I woke up energized, looking forward to the clinic. A part of me hoped for a repeat of the experience I'd had the day before but nothing of the sort happened. When we returned to the hotel, a new process started inside me and it went from bad to worse. My thoughts were fragmented and choppy, I couldn't focus on one simple thing and I prayed the night would pass and it all to be over. I went for a walk to get some fresh air and it helped me settle a bit but I was still feeling anxious and hyper. I drank and it helped but not enough, eventually I went to bed, exhausted.

Over the next few days the effects kept changing and I was tired of it. I thought perhaps it was related to my treatment at the clinic so I shared my symptoms with my doctor. He recommended a supplement to help me until I returned to London whereupon, I was advised to consult with my doctor and conduct tests. The symptoms changed and I suffered from new ones. My thoughts were overpowering, I would go into a daydream state but I ended up seeing several things at once and all with their unique sounds. It was as if there were ten television sets in my head all going off at once. I exercised and prayed, I suspected what was happening was a result of my vision. I found it very difficult to concentrate or to focus on anything specific. The sudden surge in energy meant that I was now struggling to maintain my sanity. I increased my daily workout routine at the gym, tried to sleep longer, changed my diet. Went for walks and tried to listen to music and watch some light hearted comedies. Keeping myself occupied helped to some degree, however, it was still a struggle.

I finished my treatment in Russia and flew back to London. I reflected a lot on my experience while on the plane, I could not explain any of it.

In London, I wanted to share my experience with Claudine but first I needed to get over my after effects to be able to focus and be coherent. I complained to Claudine about the side-effects such as restlessness and the excessive amount of energy that I was experiencing. I attributed them to my treatment, neither of us knew what to do. She suggested that maybe I needed to rest and over the next few days, I went for walks in the park and I found that by being in nature and close to the trees and water, I was in a better frame of mind and improved. It took some time but the intensity started clearing away and as it did, I felt sensitive to everything around me; people, pets, etc. I sensed things far more than ever before, my perception had been altered and heightened somehow. Whatever was happening to me was a result of my other worldly experience and not because of the eye treatment. I started to understand the communications that I received and their significance, I felt that something was changed in me so that I was prepared for what was to come. When I came to this realisation, I calmed down and focused and functioned as normal. It was such a great relief to be able to enjoy the quiet again.

With my sensitivity heightened, I better understood the changes in me and came to terms with them. I told Claudine about my experience at the clinic in Moscow and she appreciated it and told me to treasure it. In fact, she helped me understand the message further and explained that perhaps more would be revealed in time when I was further opened and prepared to better understand.

Claudine told me that a dear friend's son was involved in a serious car accident in Ghana. The boy R. was flown to the UK on an emergency flight, he had a life-threatening traumatic brain injury. I did not know the family but I joined Claudine on a visit to the hospital. We went by underground train and before arriving at the National Hospital for Neurology and Neurosurgery in Russel Square, my breathing became long and heavy. I felt lightheaded and slightly dizzy, I thought I was becoming ill and contemplated going home. Claudine asked me if I was okay and I said yes but I was worried, my heart was beating faster and I was feeling restless. It was as if I was desperately excited to get to the hospital and I couldn't get there quick enough.

Eventually we arrived at the hospital and I met the family in the waiting area. Each family member was being strong for the other and despite their show of strength and faith, I felt their pain. I warmed up to them. We were in the waiting area, being offered coffees, making small talk but I was desperate to go to the room where the patient was. I became restless and impatient, a powerful and overwhelming feeling was directing me, almost pulling at me to get up and go to R.'s room. I could contain myself no longer and just then to my luck, the boy's mother asked us if we wanted to visit her son in his room, I almost sprang up from my seat and I went with her and Claudine. I remember that the closer I went to the room, the heavier I felt and my heart beat even quicker in anticipation. I stood at the door and all the feelings stopped, I felt an overwhelming sense of peace, similar to when I had my experience in Russia. There was a change taking place within me, an energy of some sort was now super-imposed on me and I felt that I was being directed what to do next. On the bed lay the injured boy and he appeared to be unwell. He was rotating his arm in circles and grimacing every so often while occasionally trying to move his lips. He would then settle before repeating the same. I was sad to see him suffer and even more so for his parents who must've been devastated to see their son rendered helpless in that manner.

As I entered R.'s room, I met his grandmother who was reading the Holy Quran. I put my hand on his forehead and prayed silently. I felt a rush go through me. I could not remove my hand from the young patient's forehead, time froze, and I momentarily lost myself.

As quickly as it all started, it suddenly stopped and I became conscious of my hand on the boy's forehead so I gently pulled back. I felt embarrassed, I had taken liberty in laying my hand on the patient without asking for permission but I remember L., the boy's mother, smiling to me warmly and thanking us both for coming to see them.

We went home but mentally and emotionally I was still in hospital with R. and his family. The image of R. sprawled on the bed with repetitive head injury syndrome was painful, I could only imagine how it must have felt to his family and L. especially. I tried to occupy myself with different things but I was still unable to fully function as I normally did, my mind was still wandering in thoughts and I could not remove R. or his family from my mind.

"Are you okay? You look like you are miles away in thought," Claudine asked me. I was standing in our bedroom back at home, looking at the world outside through the window.

Till this day, I don't know what compelled me to say, "Claudine, I can help R. I need to see him again. Can you speak with his mother about healing?"

"I don't know if I can discuss this with her, I will try ... she is desperate for her son to improve."

"Listen to me, you need to speak with her about it... I can help him."

Ten minutes later, my wife's phone rang, and it was L. calling. Claudine greeted her and before she had a chance to relay my message to her, I heard my wife say the following,

"... yes he is ... this is scary, he just spoke to me about you and asked me to speak with you about it. I am lost for words. Yes, I will tell him ... no need to thank, anything we can do ... "

She turned to me and she was quite shocked. She told me that L. called to ask her if I was a healer and my wife confirmed it. L told my wife that she observed me go into the room, place my hand over her son's forehead and pray.... She sensed something taking place and felt it would be healing for her son. I was deeply touched and honoured and because I had taken a liking to the family and the boy, I felt that I would do whatever it took to help them.

That night I retired earlier than usual, and I prayed and asked for guidance. I felt doubt creeping in and I started questioning things, but I quickly dismissed these thoughts and resigned to the fact that our Lord Jesus Christ said that the power of prayer can move mountains.

I slept for a while but then woke at night and went to

the front room where I stood at the window looking at the passing cars. I could not remove the image of the poor boy from my head. I also felt a connection with his mother, she recognised my gift and I felt a deep appreciation from her.

The next day, after breakfast, I went to the hospital to venture on a life long journey, armed with nothing but faith and hope.

My journey in service as an instrument of God was about to unfold.

PATIENT R

I entered the hospital room and R. was sprawled on the bed; his condition unchanged. A nurse and his mother were dressing him. I sat to the side and waited patiently while R. went through the repetitive motions he was doing the day before. He still appeared to be unconscious and didn't respond to his name or to any words or sentences. His mother excused herself and I sat on a chair near the patient's bed, baffled, wondering why I was there, what I could possibly do for the boy. I did not know at the time that the surgeons had told his parents that there was a good possibility that R. would not wake up from his coma and even if he did, he would probably end up in a vegetative state. As I sat contemplating the enormity of the situation and feeling nervous about putting up the mother's hopes, wanting to leave, something made me stay. I was still weighing up the situation and questioning my presence when the words "Pray Garo... pray." were impressed on me. This was my cue to go ahead and pray and not to think or analyse the situation.

I went to R.'s bedside and knelt. I ignored the patient

and all the associated symptoms and his behaviour and just focused on my prayer. I prayed and asked that God grant me permission to be of service and to accept my prayers for the boy and his family. As I prayed, I felt a great calmness surround me and in contrast to the insecurity that I experienced earlier, I felt empowered and hopeful. I was no longer concerned about the enormity of the situation, nor was I worried if it was going to work or not, I made the decision that I'd do my best. With my anxieties put to one side, there was now room for peace and calm, the main ingredients for healing. I stood by the patient and slowly drifted away, I was now in my own world and away from everything and everyone around me. I do not recall everything that took place but I remember vaguely, standing by the bed and at times placing my hands on the patient, holding his hand and then placing my hand on his forehead. Eventually, I felt that I was losing my orientation, my head was heavy. The serenity was now replaced by a terrible feeling that made me feel ill, the effect changed. I cried and I don't know why. It was as if I had picked up all the pain from R. and those around him. I felt the trauma, the impact and the devastation the accident had caused. I felt the family's deep pain, the type of pain that lingers from a never ending nightmare. I picked up everything around me, saw visions and felt different emotions. I was connecting with R. and I felt that at some inexplicable level, we actually bonded. I set my mind on doing my best for him.

When in service of healing, I do not follow any techniques. I have not been trained or instructed on what to do. I just surrender myself in prayer and whatever is meant to happen will take place. Most of the time, I get a feeling and that is enough for me to follow. Sometimes, I may hear a voice in my head or even see a vision in my mind's eye. Whatever the case, I am always reminded that I am just the instrument and in service of the patient and God.

I persevered despite all odds as I distinctly felt something much higher than me at work. I am not sure why, but I even felt responsible for the boy, as if he had been entrusted to me and I had to do my best for him.

Eventually, I came back to myself and the pleasant numbness that I was feeling was quickly replaced by weakness and nausea. I wanted to leave.... I wanted to go home. I wasn't feeling well. I took my time to recover, washed my face with cold water, and fought against the nausea and everything horrible that I was feeling.

"I need to do more work here ... this is going to need time," I told his mother. She nodded in agreement and asked me if I could come back.

She walked with me the length of the corridor and thanked me for my help. I left for the train, I felt as if I was going to collapse. I should have eaten but I did not.... I was hungry but I was also feeling sick and exhausted. When I got home, I staggered to the bathroom and threw up. Afterwards, I collapsed on the bed. It was a difficult time for me and I went through many emotions. My biggest fear was of failure and of letting the family down. Part of me regretted taking on such a huge responsibility but at the same time, I felt that I was doing the honourable thing. I fought hard against every dark thought and prayed for strength.

At one point, I woke up to Claudine wiping my face with

a towel and cold water, apparently I had asked her for it. The cold water helped me settle but I was still feeling sick and threw up again. It took a long time for me to regain my strength. I was desperate for sleep. Eventually I did fall asleep and felt a bit better when I woke up.

I spent a quiet day recovering, watching television, doing some work and took a stroll in the park. I needed to get my mind off things. I am by nature quite inquisitive and if left to my own devices, I would have spent all day trying to dissect things to make sense of it all. I needed to speak with someone so I met with Paula. I described what happened with R. and she encouraged me to continue to be of service. I told her that I feared that R.'s condition may be impossible to recover from, I felt terrible for the family. I was now their hope and I did not want to let them down. Paula assured me that by simply being present at their side and by trying my best for their son, I'd be giving the family much needed support. If anything, it would be immensely comforting for them to witness the love and support for their child, they would appreciate it. I described some of the aftereffects I was going through and she explained I was probably taking the negative energies on myself and that was how my healing worked. She asked me to bear with it and focus on the invaluable service itself. She expressed her delight and reiterated to me just how valuable my presence was at the hospital and this renewed my hope. I felt assured that whatever the outcome, it would be positive. A day later I had regained enough strength to resume my service.

Before I continue further, I must explain a point which I strongly believe. Healing and science work hand-in-hand.

In fact, a professor and scientist friend once told me that where science stops, God continues. R.'s surgeons and carers were fantastic, and I doubt if they did any less than their best for their patient. R.'s healing came from both science and God.

So many people prayed for R. and his family, news of the boy travelled around the world and complete strangers prayed for him. My own mother who did not know the family lit candles and prayed for R. There was an overwhelming sense that we all needed to do whatever we could to try and save him. The energy and drive were incredible and I have no doubt that the collective well wishes and prayers had a positive impact on the family. If anything, it gave them strength to go on.

I returned to the hospital. I went to R.'s bedside, knelt and prayed. I sensed that I should look past the patient and his family and just focus on my prayers to lose myself to God's work. I could not afford to lose sight of my mission, nor should I allow myself to be distracted. When I finished my prayers, I felt the healing sensation all over and my breathing became heavier once again. I was surrounded with an incredible feeling of peace and I felt distinctly confident. That day was different. I was being directed to do certain things, I even vaguely heard instructions. Soon my vision had become hazy and foggy, I was in between two worlds. I sensed the presence of others in the room but I ignored them. My hands wandered on their own, sometimes I felt I needed to place them on R. and at other times, I was pulled away. There was yet again a distinct build-up of energy which I felt run like a current through me. In the end, I pulled away, feeling disoriented and weak. I had again taken on something from R. that was making me feel ill. I could barely walk to the waiting room and I slumped in a chair. I was offered water and I also asked for coffee, strong black. I craved something sweet and I ate a piece of chocolate.

People spoke to me and I responded mechanically. I just wanted to be left alone, I felt faded and could not really focus or fathom a thought. I wasn't in pain but I was in discomfort and later I felt nauseas and weak. I left the hospital and went home to rest, I felt depleted. I woke up feeling sick, my legs could barely carry me to the bathroom where I vomited at least twice. I went back to bed shivering and cold, I was dizzy and weak. It was all too much to bear; I fought back tears.

I reflected on what I was going though and wondered why I was being 'punished' this way. I believed in helping the boy and his family, but I was getting ill in consequence and this was affecting me physically, emotionally and spiritually. I found the sickly feeling unbearable and I did everything to try and stop it but nothing really helped. I understood that this was my path and that there was little choice but to bear with it. I tried to focus on the end result in the hope that it will all end well for the boy. I prayed and asked for help and then eventually I slept.

I woke up after seeing a vision of an older gentleman in a white robe or perhaps a frock. He had a goatee of grey hair, he was bald and with hair on either side of his head. He said,

"You walk with us now … " I couldn't understand his final word.

I thought about what I had seen and heard but I went back to sleep. I woke to find Claudine at home.

"You do not look good … are you okay? Shall I get you something?" she asked.

I did not tell her just how bad I was feeling but there was no fooling her. She fetched me some food and some juice. I hardly ate and went back to sleep. I woke up soon after and could not decide whether to sleep or just stay as I was. I could not focus.

"I don't feel good Claudine; I don't know how I will go through with this."

She was concerned and did not know what to say. We were quiet for a while, I did not intend to worry her, there was little that could be done, I had to bear with it…. Quitting was not an option.

That night I had a significant dream. In it, I came out of the elevator on the ground floor at our block where I was met with a young girl who looked quite anxious. She said, "I am sorry to intrude on you but you are Garo aren't you?"

"Yes, I am, who are you?"

"It's about my father, he is ill with cancer, he needs help. Please, is there anything that you can do?"

It dawned on me that she was the daughter of a certain

person who had wronged my wife Claudine and caused her distress. I was angry with that person and disliked him.

"Please Garo, if there is anything that you can do for my father, he may not have long...."

I agreed to see him, and she thanked me again and again.

The dream ended and I felt it was the right decision to help. The message followed: *God's love is unconditional, you must serve indiscriminately. You are to receive no material reward for your service, nor should you accept it. You will receive no recognition, and nor should you expect it. Do not seek your value in others, you will not find it. This is your path.*

When I woke up, I reflected on the dream and I understood its meaning. I was being prepared to be of service to anyone who healing was intended for and not to allow my personal views or feelings to affect any part of the process. I could see how things were now falling into place. I was going through a major change and I must be prepared for what was ahead. This was a big responsibility, and I was worried about messing it up. The question 'why me?' was on my mind. I kept wondering why I would be selected for this sort of service. I am not a regular churchgoer. Nor am I devoutly religious, although I do respect God and all religions. I enjoy the finer things in life and at a personal level I can be difficult and even a real pain sometimes. I am not usually a social person and I am only comfortable around small numbers of people. My sins, if stacked up, could easily dwarf the Eiffel Tower. There are devoted and religious individuals in the world who are far worthy candidates than I am so why me? I could not find an answer and I tried hard to make sense of things but eventually I gave up and continued attending to R. at the hospital. Paula helped me simplify things and not over-analyse the situation. I learnt to accept that I may not be a worthy candidate in my own eyes but in God's eyes, we are all perceived for who we really are. So, who was I to judge?

The message that followed my dream set the guidelines clearly.

A couple weeks went by and I saw changes in R. One day I was alone with him and he was in a chair an arm's length from me. He raised his head and we briefly locked eyes. For the first time ever, I felt a sense of unmistakable awareness from him and I was thrilled, I called his mother and told her to speak with him like normal and she did. It was a moving sight, seeing her caress his forehead and kiss him, telling him she loved him and that he will be all right. I felt at that instant that despite all odds, R. would be healed by the grace of God.

That night at around 3 a.m. I awoke to a strange loud noise, it was someone or something speaking and the voice was terrifying, it did not sound human and it was angry. There was no one in the room apart from my wife. I quickly reached over to put the bedside light on but my hand was trembling as I fumbled with the switch. The voice continued even when I put the light on. I heard a distinct menacing voice, mechanical and downright evil in fact.

"We will break every bone in your body, you will see.... We will break you. We will break you! You just wait and see...."

Expletives followed the warning. I was terrified of the voice and accidentally wet myself. I undressed to shower but first I had to check on Claudine who I found to be fast asleep. How could she not have heard it? I know I did not imagine it.

My hands shook as I showered. I felt angry because I was so vulnerable, this was a serious warning and I knew exactly why I received it. I sat in the living room, alone, trying to distract myself from thinking about the warning. I wasn't worried about myself, I was worried for Claudine and my parents. For the first time since I chose to be in service, I felt that I had made the wrong choice. I couldn't wait for the morning to come so I could call Paula and get her advice.

Paula was calm and listened to me describe my ordeal.

"Unfortunately Garo, when you do God's work, you will become a target of such attacks, it is expected!"

"I cannot get that voice out of my head Paula. I am worried for my loved ones."

"Your loved ones are protected, don't worry about them. You are doing good work in service of humanity, you will be looked after, they will also be looked after."

Despite her reassurance, I was still afraid and I felt deeply sad to have put everyone I love in harm's way. I was also upset not to have been forewarned about the possible dangers and difficulties ahead. I did not rule out the existence of the darker elements, but it did not cross my mind that in being of service, I would attract new enemies who would want to see me stop at all costs. Fear was their advantage and I would be lying if I were to say that I wasn't afraid. On my way home, I watched people going about their business. I was an outsider, detached from the mainstream mechanics of life. I was the loneliest person on the planet. Why was I different? Why could I not be just a regular person who goes to work, comes back home, meets with friends in the pub, etc. I never fit in at school or college and now it seems I still didn't belong, no matter how hard I tried. In fact, if anything, I was now more detached from the mainstream than ever before. I was desperately seeking sanity after a much turbulent past and yet I found myself at the deep end; scared and alone. So many thoughts swarmed through my head. I was being punished for my decision to serve as a healer, with the only consolation being that I was not alone. I told my wife about my experience but I could not share it in detail. I did not want to scare her but she figured it out anyway. When I went back to the hospital, I was greeted warmly by R.'s mother. He'd been making good progress on a daily basis. Seeing how her eyes were lighting up at the prospect of hope for her son and upon entering the room and being greeted by R., I felt a surge go through me. The dark side may break every bone in my body, but it couldn't take away that special moment. I prayed for guidance and strength and decided that I'd continue to be in service to R. and whoever needed my help. I did not give a damn anymore....

I continued my work with R., going to hospital to see him every other day. I met other members of his warm family and I particularly remember his aunt 'I'. My healing sessions resumed in the presence of her who took over for

R.'s mother at times. She was of great help to me and R. I do not recall much of what happened, the sessions were deeper and more intense and I would always drift away on a mini journey into a different realm in the process. I once had a chat with 'I' over a coffee and she told me that while I was healing R. she tried to look at me but could not because of a bright light surrounding me. It was reassuring to hear but more rewarding was the fact that R. was improving at an accelerated rate and was now able to speak. He took me by surprise when he greeted me with a 'Hi' as I entered his hospital room. I will never forget that moment, it was magical It was the beginning of my deep friendship with R.

I was witnessing a miracle unfold, and I was honoured to play a part in it. We do not often get a chance to do something so good. Perhaps I was being offered a chance to redeem myself from my sinful and foolish ways of the past, I don't know. That same day a group of nurses who were attending to R. in A&E visited him in his room while I was there. As soon as they entered, the head nurse made the sign of the cross.

"Oh my God ... " they exclaimed, shocked to see R. alive and recovering. He was upright in his bed and greeted them when they entered. We were all delighted and many tears flowed on that day.

My experience with the threat that I received was quickly becoming a distant memory. I decided to resume my service regardless, not in defiance but because I chose to do the right thing. Besides, I was becoming sick and tired of fear being used against me. I grew up in fear and it had affected me throughout my life. I was also motivated by principle. Sometimes, we receive confirmations in the most bizarre ways but they are messages that are important for us as we go through different stages of our lives. I was at the train station, when I found the message scrawled on a wall. In life, if you do not stand for something, you will bend for anything.

The time had come for me to take a stand against fear.

One day when I finished my healing service at the hospital, I felt the need to go to a nearby park. There I sat on the ground and leant against an old tree. I closed my eyes and drifted away in a dream state and I saw in my mind's eye a beautiful sight. A canvas was pulsating with vibrant colours surrounded by a majestic white light and shimmering gold. I could feel my back against the tree and my hands clutching at the grass. I was in command but at the same time, I had surrendered myself to what I could best describe as heaven. It was so beautiful, no words could ever do it justice. I am not sure why I saw this vision but if it was meant to be a treat then it was well received.

Then I drifted even deeper and eventually saw a different vision of an old man sitting on a rock. It was the same old man whom I had seen before, dressed in a white robe or frock. The ocean was behind him and the full moon reflected on his face and surroundings. The man stared at me with a warm and gentle smile. He communicated silently by telepathy, but only much deeper. I can no longer remember what was communicated to me in full but soon a lady appeared from the side. She was excited to see me and she spoke in a calm and reassuring tone

"It is beautiful Garo.... It is beautiful." I was thrilled but I also had no idea who they were.

She moved away again and I was left looking at the man in the white robe sitting on the rock. He did not say anything but I felt his warm energy and calming thoughts. There was an air of familiarity around him. He purposely gazed at me, he wanted me to know who he was and slowly I felt a strong impression of his identity and that he was one of the twelve disciples of Christ. I was overwhelmed, but not too surprised given the fact that R. made such a miraculous recovery.

I snapped out of the dream state and returned to my surroundings in the park. It took me some time to regain my earthly senses and to get up and leave. I felt so relaxed, I just wanted to stay under that tree, enjoying the incredible moment.

The question Why me? kept coming to mind.

I looked around and saw people drinking and enjoying social functions and here I was digesting a difficult revelation. I wanted to be one of the normal people and just to get on with a normal life but it was not to be. I was excited about this latest revelation but I got the distinct feeling I had to keep it to myself at the time and I did just that. I imagined that my experience was bound to receive ridicule. Things have changed since then and I am now at liberty to reveal things.

Paula picked up on that I was stressed about something and I felt confident enough to share my vision and the revelation with her. She was happy about it and using her own perception and from what I described, she eventually identified the disciple in question. However, she also encouraged me to put it behind me and not to be swayed by names or titles, under God, we are all equal. This helped me tremendously as I was finding myself again being influenced by the status of my communicator and this would be detrimental to my work and my state of mind. I took home the fact that I was deeply honoured to be in service and to be playing a positive role in people's lives for a change.

The healing sessions with R. continued and they were profound. The family trusted me wholeheartedly and R. surrendered himself in the hope that he would walk again. I assured him that he would and even nicknamed him Mr. Tarzan.

A week later, I went to hospital and R. was not in his room. His mother and other family members greeted me with excitement, they said that he was walking! Apparently the nurses took him out for a walk in the corridor. I waited for him and then he eventually appeared back at his room, cane in hand and with no human support. He was slightly wobbly but he managed to walk up to me.

"Hello Mr. Tarzan," he called out to me "I can walk again!"

"Oh no ... God help us all!"

He loved my reply and laughed.

We started our healing session and I thanked God for R.'s

improvements. We were alone when I started the healing and R. started asking me very deep questions.

"Why did this happen to me Garo?"

"I don't know R. I wish I knew, and I wish it never happened to you." He then went on to curse God a few times and quickly apologized. I assured him that the Creator of the universe would not be bothered by mere words and especially coming from someone who was unwell.

"Do you think God would be angry with me if I was to say something bad about him?"

"No. God understands that you are angry, and this is why he is helping you get better."

"Do you think I will be able to run again?"

"Yes, you will ... it will take a bit longer, but you will run and do things that others do and more...."

"How do you know?"

"I just feel it...."

"Garo, do you have super powers?"

"No, I don't. I wish I did though!"

"What do you do?"

"I pray R. I just pray for people to get better."

R. appreciated what I did, and I felt we connected somehow. He understood without me having to explain much. R. was an intuitive and sensitive soul. He trusted me wholeheartedly and it helped a lot that he did. He fought to get better and was ready to do anything, whatever it took. R. was and still is our inspiration, he never gave up and the blessed angels never gave up on him either.

R.'s condition continued to improve very quickly. One day, while working with him, I got the distinct feeling that the session was to be heavy. I drifted away but unlike other sessions, I felt as if I fell asleep during the session. Eventually when I came round, I wanted to go home. I could not link to people around me, I was in two worlds and it was all hazy and out of sync. R. was asleep and I felt ill, I had to rush home. I fell asleep and when I woke up, I discovered that I was out for more than a day and a half. It took a great effort for me to return to this reality and to be in control of myself. I could not focus on my surroundings, I could not eat or drink properly and the nauseous feeling followed me even when I threw up. I felt trapped in a stale and sickening energy and I could not get rid of it. I tried everything, from visualisation to prayer. At one point I closed my eyes in bed and saw my communicator's face, his smile, I felt that I should bear with it, I would get better soon. Although it gave me hope, I still struggled and contemplated ceasing from this responsibility. I genuinely wanted to help others but perhaps it was time for me to reconsider my position as a healer. I was not getting any benefit from the process, which I was prepared to accept but there is an added challenge here and that is dealing with the after effects and consequences of my service. Even though I felt confused and at odds with myself, I could never give up healing. It was my calling, my mission... I had to serve. Other healers recommended that I do certain things to avoid the ill effects, but I felt that they were unavoidable and Paula confirmed it.

This was the heaviest session and I could not return to the hospital for a few days. When I did go back, I took a chess set with me. I have no idea what inspired me, but I felt that it would be fun. I was astonished to see just how much R. had improved since I last saw him. We hugged and he shook my hand firmly to demonstrate how tough he was. I asked R. if he wanted to play a game of chess and we sat together on the bed and played. A nurse walked in and was flabbergasted to see R. playing chess. Others from his medical team who followed were equally awed.

R. continued to improve until one day, I went to the hospital and when I started my prayers, I could not feel the warm fuzzy energy that I had become accustomed to. I did not drift away, but stayed wide awake and mentally present. I knew there and then that my service had come to an end. I informed R.'s parents and they thanked me with warm hugs and kisses. I was deeply touched but also honoured, I felt that for once in my life I had actually done something right and seen it through.

When I went home, I sat alone trying to make sense of all that had happened but no matter which way I thought of it, I just couldn't come to terms with it. This was a level that was well beyond me and definitely not something that I ever expected. It was hard for me not to become fascinated by everything that took place and the attention that I received was also overwhelming. As the days went by, I found myself missing going to the hospital and missing the family, above all I missed my new friend R. and thought of him often. I met with Paula and over a strong black coffee she helped me with the following insight:

"Your work is finished with this family but there will be others, many others. It will always be hard to pull away from those who you help because your work comes from love, but you will learn. As hard as it may appear to be the case now, you will get used to it."

"I miss going to the hospital, I miss the healing sessions.... I was completely at peace knowing that I was part of something so immense, so incredible."

"You served a purpose and that is what will stay with you forever. There will be others Garo. All in good time."

She was right, there have been many others since. Every patient and situation are unique, but the bottom line is that some fascinating results have been witnessed and achieved.

My work with R. was extremely rewarding for me at many levels, I learnt a lot about myself and others through the process. Most of all, I learnt from the champion himself, R., who despite every challenge, kept his faith and belief strong. R. now attends university where he excels in his studies. He is determined on improving himself at all levels and his tragic accident continues to be his drive; to learn from and to conquer endless possibilities and challenges. I am honoured to be part of his life as much as he is a part of mine.

After this particular experience I found myself adrift in different directions. For a while, I lost myself to the thought that I was 'the healer' and I succumbed to vanity and self-importance. It was hard not to be affected by the attention I received and I found myself battling inner conflicts trying to keep myself grounded but it was difficult sometimes. This was a weakness within me which I identified over the years but as my confidence grew I matured sufficiently not to allow myself to be dazzled by what is going on during the healing process and not to claim credit for any aspect of my service. It took experience, discipline and dedication and in time I learnt. It was vital that I did not knowingly or unknowingly obstruct the healing process in any way. I would never forgive myself if I was the reason for its failing.

I travelled to my home country, Lebanon, and stayed there for a little while and it was during my visit that I discovered that my path was to take a new turn. With most of my inner battles resolved, I was ready for a new one. I unwittingly ventured into the world of exorcism and the clearance of unwanted dark energies, demons and entities.

A memorable and touching communication came through from my communicator and I will treasure it forever:

"You are of us, as we are of you."

PATIENT P. EXORCISM

I've been fascinated by exorcism from a young age. Having watched the movie 'The Exorcist' and after reading on the subject in various publications, I found the subject to be simply incredible. This was the ultimate battle of earthly good over otherworldly evil; a battle of two worlds. I was scared of the subject, the thought that humans are susceptible to malevolent or demonic force terrified me. What made it even more horrific is when I discovered that the movie 'The Exorcist' was apparently based on real-life events from an exorcism performed on a young boy.

I was once taken over by two entities and later saved by an exorcist, so I had a rough idea and a vivid recollection of what it was like to be at the receiving end of entity encroachment. It's one of the most torturous experiences anyone can go through. It not only affects the patient but also their loved ones, family and friends, as they witness an ugly transformation and a mystifying regression that imminently leads to a complete personality change. I have not witnessed an exorcism as dramatic as what was portrayed in the movies but what I have experienced so far has been a catalogue of pain and suffering and patients driven into despair. I never thought the day would come when I myself would become an exorcist. I guess our paths guide us towards who we truly are and not who we imagine ourselves to be.

Patient P. was the sister of a family friend. I was told about her condition and that she was poor in health, she was having regular dialysis treatments due to her failing kidneys. According to her family, P. suffered from different ailments. There was no consistency in her life with extreme swings between ill health and basic survival. My sister had discussed my healing with her friend and the patient's family were keen that I visit her, hoping that I could make a positive difference. I arrived on the scheduled day and was greeted warmly by her mother, a special lady of love and faith. P. looked weak and lacked colour in her skin and her sunken eyes spoke of deep sadness and suffering. After some social chat, I began my prayers and surrendered myself in commencement of the healing service. It was an ordinary day and I did not feel that anything special occurred during the session. In fact, I thought it odd that I did not feel any of the usual effects associated with my healing work, it was all pretty routine. I left the patient and went home wondering why the healing energy that I felt on previous occasions was absent. I thought about it over the next few days when I heard that the patient had become ill again. I called to check on her and was invited to her home.

I went back late afternoon the next day. I felt slightly awkward when I arrived at the apartment because I was convinced that nothing of significance had happened on my previous visit. I had been made aware in the past that healing will only be of benefit to those who are meant to be healed. Perhaps this patient was one of the less fortunate ones and not destined for recovery, I did not know. I certainly did not want to waste the patient's time or put her hopes up. I reflected on my experience with patient R. and on how I was told not to analyse and just pray. I closed my eyes and opened the session with a prayer and eventually I felt myself drift away. I did not experience anything noteworthy for a short while and then all of a sudden I saw an image in my mind's eye that stayed for some time. I was looking at barren land, where severe drought had caused the ground to crack in multiple places. The backdrop was dark with little light which appeared to streak from above. I couldn't see the source of illumination, it was neither the moon nor any stars. The setting was the background for an entity who now stood in the foreground, staring at me. It did not communicate in any way and remained absolutely still. It looked like a cross between human and goat, it had long goat-like horns. Its features were dark so I could not distinguish its features but from what I could see, it appeared as a beast of some sort, a biblical demon type and it felt powerful. Yet it remained inanimate and I was not receiving any communication from it so I decided to shift my focus elsewhere but the harder I tried, the harder it was to remove the image from my head. I was weary of the fact that whatever this creature was, it could at any time come out of its 'frozen state' and cause serious damage. I did not understand the significance of seeing the image of a beast and it started making me feel uneasy. What was this vision that I was seeing and why was I seeing it? What was the meaning behind it? I felt protected, I wasn't afraid. I prayed for guidance.

There was a distinct difference in this healing session, I have never experienced a vision such as this. Something was making me stay still and I was frozen in the same position for a while. I am unsure for how long exactly but it seemed for a long time. I then started to come out of the light trance and when I came round, I felt physically sick and I started to cough. My chest felt heavy and it was hard to breath. I felt weak and claustrophobic; I needed to get out of that room. The symptoms were different from previous ones. I was feeling ill spiritually more so than physically. I excused myself and went to the bathroom. I washed my face with cold water, hoping that it would help settle me down. I felt an overwhelming sense of entrapment, desperately wanting to get out of that apartment. My breathing became heavier, I felt the walls around me were closing in on me.

On my way back to the front room where my patient and family were waiting, I saw an older man enter from what I presumed was the kitchen. He was in his pyjamas and looked frail and shuffled along but I felt that there was more to him and I got the distinct feeling not to engage with him. We stood staring at each other for a little while and no words were exchanged. I found it strange that the man did not greet me or even enquire as to who I was. The encounter was borderline confrontational and we both did not say anything. I sensed his fear and a darkness around him; this man had been touched by evil, I could see it in his eyes. I wasn't sure who he was exactly but I assumed he was P.'s father. While the mother was warm in every way, the man standing before me made me feel uncomfortable and I wanted him out of my way. I got the distinct feeling that he was unhappy about my presence in the house. Ordinarily, I would have politely introduced myself but on this occasion I just stood my ground facing him and stared back until he moved on.

In time, I learnt to look for the smallest pieces of puzzles to complete a larger picture, the old man played a significant role and had impact on my patient's wellbeing. When he left, I re-entered the front room where P. and her family were waiting for me. I proceeded with the healing and removed the thought of the man from my mind. When I reflect on the memory of the old man in the darkened corridor, the only way I can describe it is 'spooky'.

I placed one hand on P.'s back and the other on her shoulder. Shortly after, the image of the beast I'd seen earlier came to my mind and this time I saw other images, choppy and disconnected, everything was happening so quickly, I was unable to make sense of things and was becoming confused and frustrated. I got the impression that I should brace myself for what was to come, I wasn't sure what exactly I was waiting for but I waited as guided to do so. Gradually, with every breath, I became detached from my surroundings and although I knew that for a fact I was physically in the room, part of me felt as if I was in a different setting, at a different location and vibration. This was a new feeling that I hadn't experienced and to describe it as 'strange' would be an understatement. Maybe I was lucky to have been oblivious to what was to come next, the root of the patient's problem.

I entered what I can best describe as a mental whirlwind, then the visions suddenly stopped and I felt a surge go through me and I was overwhelmed with so many emotions, most prominently was the feeling of despair and entrapment. I started to shake, first my right hand and then the left. I was struggling to speak and it was becoming increasingly harder for me to control my thoughts. I wanted to scream! I felt enveloped by something and I was quickly losing my identity and my thoughts were turning dark. The feeling of entrapment was strong and I was desperate for it to end but it was getting worse. I felt that there was no way out and that I was stuck. I started to struggle against something that had become embedded in me and with every second, I was weaker. I panicked, not knowing if this was ever going to end. I heard voices, all speaking at once in menacing tones. I tried to pull myself out of this state but I couldn't. I couldn't regain my control and I feared that I was losing my mind, it certainly felt like it.

When I managed to briefly gather my thoughts, I got the impression that I'd taken the patient's negative energy into me. I didn't know I'd taken in an entity which had now become trapped inside me. I remember seeing the concern on the family members' faces. I felt the urge to get some fresh air and I stumbled towards the open window behind me. I looked into the night and observed the city light. I stood still and just continued breathing in and out of the window. My breathing intensified and slowly regained myself. I felt lighter; the cool fresh air was a welcome relief. I focused on my own identity and kept hold of it so that I can stop wandering into confusion, I slowly felt assured; the overwhelming entity that had taken over me was deserting me as if it was being pulled away from me. I was relieved but also worried about what had happened. I was too tired to think about it, I just experienced something that was completely alien to me, it worried me but I had to be strong for my patient. I wanted to go home, I was drained and I needed time alone.

The experience was so overwhelming, it took time for me to put it behind me and to move on from it. I found myself daydreaming and seeing the entity and the more I thought of it the more anxious I became. I understood what had happened, but I was surprised that it did. I was also grateful to have been spared after a brush with evil, this close. The experience shook me, it was not pleasant, but I was glad that it was over and done with.

I flew back to London not too long after that episode and settled back to my personal life. My wife and I were starting the process of IVF treatment and so I shifted my focus away from all other responsibilities to support Claudine. Unfortunately after a lot of effort, time and money, the IVF failed and we sad. The junior doctor at the clinic put our hopes high, so when we the devastating news, I could no longer hold myself together for my wife and I slowly sank into depression. I doubted my sanity and my faith and felt angry and resentful for not being blessed with a child. This was the hardest test of our sanity and faith, it wasn't easy but we managed to pull through it eventually. During this time, I drifted away from my healing work. I needed time to myself, away from everything and everyone.

Eventually we recovered and I knew that I had to continue in my healing service. Although I hurt deeply inside, I could not deny others the benefit of the gift. This took a lot of hard work and effort to accept on my part; to be in service of God and yet being deprived of a child. This was my dichotomy for a long time but with help from Paula and also my communicator, I was able to slowly claw my way back into the church and resume my healing service. I asked Paula why my wife and I were unable to have a child after all the good work we'd done, but she didn't know. Her honest reply helped me come to terms with things. My communicator appeared in a vision and showed me an arena where men and women were kneeling down, praying and singing hymns while lions circled them, ready to devour them. The image was of devout Christians being fed to lions during Roman times. They died for their beliefs in Christ and his teachings, the ultimate sacrifice. His message humbled me and also empowered me, it gave me hope to stay strong and to believe in the greater good. After all, others sacrificed far more and maintained their faith even when thrown to the lions. My communicator's message was brief.

"Keep your faith strong, son"

I came to terms with the fact that a baby is a gift and I rid myself of the sense of entitlement. It wasn't easy to accept the fact that undeserving child abusers have children and we didn't, but I had to move on to plan ahead for our future. Ironically, it was when we adopted this attitude, events changed in our lives and on our last IVF trial we were blessed with our lovely daughter Taline.

When I felt better emotionally, I resumed my healing service and visited patients all over London. Most of the cases were routine and I do not recall many challenging cases, quite the contrast from what I had been involved with. Still it was a good opportunity to help others and release some of my energy. Being blessed with a child, changed me inside and I became determined to surrender myself in service to God and the patients. This was a turning point in my life, my daughter's arrival took away the anger and pain and she filled our hearts with joy.

When the dust of having a baby settled somewhat and Claudine did not need my help, I went to the Heath in Hampstead and sat in my favourite bench, facing the calming and placid lake, I prayed to God and thanked him and the blessed angels. I felt a beautiful calmness and let myself go. I went into a daydreaming state and I saw my communicator.

"Son, there is no bigger honour than being in the service of God and mankind."

With that, I broke down and sobbed. I did not care if I was alone or not, I had been carrying a heavy load for a long time and I no longer cared to hold it back anymore. All the memories started to come to my mind, my life, my past ... the more I remembered, the more I cried. Eventually, I regained my composure and walked away from the bench and as I walked towards the gate, I remembered that my communicator had addressed me as 'son' for the first time. It was so endearing, and it warmed my heart.

The light that was slowly flickering in my heart, was re-kindled and shone once again.

On my next visit to Lebanon, I met with P.'s family at a

social function. They asked me why I had not continued to see P. because she was asking about me. I explained that I wasn't feeling confident that I had made much of a difference. I asked if they were happy with my visits as I had not heard back them. They looked at each other, lost for words. Then her brother-in-law put his arm around my shoulder and drew me away for privacy. His wife joined us and they revealed the unthinkable.

"Before you visited P. and did what you did, she was living in torment. She'd wake up at night to the bed moving and shaking. Invisible hands prodding her, hitting her and slapping her. She was being physically attacked. We tried everything, but nothing worked until you did whatever you did and then it all stopped. She was finally able to sleep and to live her life without any disturbances. You gave her peace, Garo."

I stood there taking it all in—socked, but also overjoyed that my healed had made P.'s life more bearable. This was proof to me that healing operates independently of me, the healer. I do not get to choose which issues or ailments will be addressed. Healing will always find its way to those who it is intended for and in a manner that is chosen for them. I was also taken aback by the fact that I was now operating at a different level; I exorcised a dark entity from my patient. I realized that with the power of prayer I can also serve as an exorcist. In time, I discovered that through prayer, I can remove curses, spells, magic and clear haunted homes and disturbances at many levels. The power of prayer is limitless and is deeply profound when used for the benefit of others. Ordinarily, I would not classify exorcism as healing, but it is in a sense because after the process is completed patients receive long-awaited peace. Another lesson I learnt was that I should stop classifying things that are simply beyond my comprehension. Only the patient's wellbeing and restoration matter.

I was assured that my patient was in good form, so after spending quality time with my parents in Lebanon, I organized my travel back to London at the earliest date possible. I had to speak to Paula about this latest development. I desperately needed confirmation and some sort of guidance as I was slightly apprehensive, I was never braced for this sort of work and dealing with things of this nature. My life was taking too many new turns, it was impossible to keep up with the changes.

Back in London and over a steaming black coffee, I shared my experience with Paula. I felt relieved to speak to someone without being judged or dismissed. She listened to my story with great interest.

"It appears from what you described that this poor woman was being seriously interfered with by an entity or possibly even more. The entity has either attached itself to the woman or may have partially taken her over and you exorcised her of this demon."

"Do you think it is even human? I saw a beast with goat-like horns."

"I think I can relate to what you are saying.... The image is not unfamiliar to me either."

"You mean to say that you have seen this thing yourself?"

"Oh yes. I am aware of it and it is a powerful entity. You were brave!"

"I wasn't brave, I simply had no choice. If I was told what I to expect, I may have run away!"

She laughed and after a brief pause asked me how I was feeling. I told her I was scared and she understood. I explained to her that I was not comfortable being in a position where I was dealing with such things. This type of service requires nerves of steel and frankly, I am not one for it.

"With your gift and your faith, you will be called on to attend to many similar issues in the future."

"Are you sure?"

"If I thought otherwise, I would not have told you what I just did. There is more to come ... S." he shook her head. "Much more to come!"

She was right. My life was changing quickly, I was no longer the same person. In fact, I wasn't sure who I was anymore. My dreams, my aspirations, everything was changing and I was having to make the biggest sacrifices, fighting my inner demons and temptation. I drifted in thought and remembered my family, my father, the family business ... everything that I was, was changing, everything was becoming a memory. It was hard to pull away from my parents, my siblings, I wanted to be part of their lives and for them to be part of mine. But I couldn't see a way forward with my spiritual mission if I was living in Lebanon; I would not be accepted. There was also the security which money brings and I was being steered away from it but fortunately, my father was of great support and helped me whenever I asked, even when he was unaware of my calling in life.

The real challenge was that I was becoming involved with things I felt were out of my league. I valued and respected healing, but exorcism is a totally different thing involving the confrontation of dark energies, entities or worse. To battle against them without fear required unshakeable faith.

I left with a sinking feeling, I was still worried despite Paula's reassurance. I reflected on my experience with P. and tried to recollect what happened when I was confronted by that demonic entity. I was surprised that I was not afraid at the time, maybe I was naïve or silly to ignore the obvious. Whatever it was, I was being steered in a different direction, and knowledge does not necessarily always bring power.

What a far cry from my now distant dream; I wanted to be the one with psychic powers to impress others. I never wanted to be any part of having to deal with dark and evil entities. Nor could I have ever envisioned that I was to become an exorcist and rid people of dark entities and energies. When I went home later that day, I occupied my mind with different things to keep me from over thinking and analysing. My wife and I had a talk and she became concerned and asked if I was in danger. I assured her that I wasn't, but we both felt uneasy. I told her we needed to be strong in faith and put our trust in God. She made me promise that I would be careful and I assured her several times that I would. Needless to say, we both knew that there were to be difficult times ahead.

The next day I went for a walk and it was beautiful outside. The park was lush green and all sorts of flowers were blossoming. I found a secluded spot and sat alone under a tree. I listened to music, ate a sandwich and observed people playing in the distance, children running and enjoying the park. Eventually, I closed my eyes to feel the lazy cool wind on my face and in the silence, I drifted away. I saw my communicator in my mind's eye and he addressed the issue that was troubling me. He told me that my faith should be solid in the face of adversity, only then can evil be defeated. His appearance gave me strength which I desperately needed. I did have faith in God, but I was also scared and I was torn between fear and faith. My biggest issue at the time was trusting in God because I'd known many people who placed their trust in God and yet their prayers were never answered. What made me any different? Yet the words of my communicator about me having faith strong in the face of evil touched me deeply. I guess, it also meant that my trust should be strong; faith and trust go hand-in-hand. He ended his communication by reminding me of the number of people who went as far as to give their lives in faith and sacrifice for the greater good, they did so honourably. On a humorous side, I communicated back and said that this was not the path that I wanted and he smiled and replied back, "Do you think any of us chose our paths?"

I stood and dusted my clothes, appreciating that it wasn't a case of 'let someone else do it'. It was a privilege to be in service. The responsibility was great but equally important was that helped sufferers who had no one else. I couldn't imagine walking away or turning my back on them.

That evening over dinner and a cheerful drink with my wife, she teased me about something that would ultimately help me a lot in my quest.

"You do realise that part of the reason why you were chosen for this type of work is because you can be really nasty and cold when you want to be?"

"You think so?"

"I know so!" She laughed. "I am serious though, ordinarily you are a gentleman but you are also perfectly capable of being nasty when you want to be. Let's not forget your sense of humour so maybe that is something that you have to tap into. You know you are a cheeky prankster at heart!"

"So be myself really, isn't that what you're saying?"

"Yes, absolutely. I think you should not take things too seriously."

"I could never live with myself if anything was to happen to you."

"You told me that you have been assured and that we will all be safe."

"Yes"

"Then I don't see why you should be worrying about anything. Just do what you need to do and help those in need."

The next day, I committed myself and it was the start of my journey as an exorcist, a different level of healing. I had to be prepared mentally, emotionally and spiritually so I took time to focus on all three aspects of my life to be prepared for that which we can never be prepared for. It was a big decision and I had to think about it carefully. I considered Paula and felt that if I did not help others as an exorcist then who would? There is a shortage of exorcists all over the world at a time when the number of sufferers is at the highest. I had to put my fears to one side and stop thinking about the concept of exorcism and the associated mental imageries. I imagined exorcists to have unwavering faith and incredible courage but learnt that this was not necessarily the case; we are human after all. Any exorcist would be foolish to undermine any form of possession. Despite my mental focus, prayers and inner discipline, time would show just how unprepared I truly was.

AFRICAN EXPERIENCE

My wife was born and was raised in Ghana, West Africa. She invited me to Accra to visit my in-laws and meet the extended family. I had never been to Africa and I did not know what to expect.

After various family functions and get togethers, my wife suggested that we go on a sight-seeing tour. A close friend loaned us his car and driver and after preparing for a long journey, we set off to explore the different sights starting with spectacular beaches and natural parks. I had never been on a hanging bridge before and it was quite an experience to cross one as it swayed from side-to-side over a dense jungle inhabited by different creatures. Earlier that day, while on tour, we spotted a cobra as we walked in the jungle and held our breaths when it crossed our path.

When we completed our tour, we settled down at a local hotel and spent the night relaxing and savouring local cuisine and listening to music.

The next day we were driven to Cape Coast to visit Al Mina Castle. This was a castle that also doubled as a dungeon, and it is where the captives were kept prior to being shipped to various continents to be sold as slaves. It was a long drive to Cape Coast but we enjoyed the scenery, the villages and the natural beauty. When we finally arrived, I got out of the car and just looked ahead at the imposing castle majestically sitting by the side of the ocean. Cape Coast is a quaint picturesque fishing village that could easily pass for a painting. Rows of fishing boats lazily sway from side to side near the shore as fishermen load them with fishing nets in preparation of their evening fishing excursion. There are traditional markets and shops selling all manners of commodities, including clothing, food and other necessities. It was breezy and the winds carried distant singing, it was the fishermen and it was absolutely captivating.

We were met by a tour guide and we joined a group to be taken round the castle. The ground floor was made up of prison cells, dungeons and dark passages. The cells were probably no more than twelve by five meters. There were no facilities whatsoever and no windows, just iron bar doors that were the only source of air and light. The cells were damp, dark and confined. I thought that having ten captives in there would be pushing it but I was shocked to hear that they used to shove no less than a hundred prisoners in one cell. How could anyone survive this? It was horrific.

Men were separated from women but both sexes were treated with the same level of cruelty and inhumanity. The cells served a dual purpose, the first being as space for holding captives but the second more important reason was to break down the prisoners physically, mentally and spiritually so they became manageable when loading onto vessels and during their journeys on the open seas. The strategy and implementation were simple: starve the prisoners to weaken them so that they could not fight back, weaken them so they lose the will to fight and can be easily led to their final destination with the least amount of resistance. When the prisoners were ready to be shipped, they were led down a dark passage by their captors to be hauled on to waiting ships. We walked through the passage which was referred to as 'the passage of no return' and I immediately felt a heaviness and a distinct feeling of claustrophobia and anxiety. I did not want to be there but I felt that I had to honour the victims by going through the dark passage. There was a group of us and we all walked solemnly in semi-darkness with only a visible source of light from the room ahead. The passage led to a circular room with an opening on the side wall from which we could see the ocean. The guide explained that the captives were led into this room and shoved through the small opening in the wall on to the waiting ships. Those who would not go through, were taken back to prison to be further starved and brought back to the same room after some time and this process went on until they could go through the narrow opening.

I stood frozen in silence and listened to what was being recounted, yet my mind and my feelings were already elsewhere. In my mind's eye, I witnessed everything, I saw the poor souls being prodded into the room by the Portuguese soldiers carrying with sticks and bayonets. I heard the desperate wailing of the slaves as they realised the reason they were being led into that room. It was indeed the point of no return but at many different levels. They were about to be uprooted from their homes, their families, their country and all that they had once cherished. The final image of their beloved homeland was the small opening from where the sun shone through and which led to a waiting ship where they'd be stuffed in lower decks. I saw at least two Portuguese soldiers with whips in their hands, lashing out at captives and forcing them through the opening in the wall. The vision was so clear, it was as if I had actually been transported back in time and was witnessing the event in real time. I remember their uniforms and the distinct shouts and the musky smell of the room, the cracking of the whips and the screams of the terrified captives.

What happened next took me by surprise, I found myself loudly describing what I was seeing to the tour guide. I rushed through the description without even thinking of what I was saying. I don't know what the others in the group thought, but I wasn't focusing on them. I was in between two worlds and I was simply relaying what I was seeing. The tour guide confirmed what I was saying. I even pointed to the spots where the soldiers were positioned as they cracked their whips, kicked and pushed the captives to force them to go through the gap in the wall. The slaves were terrified, having no idea what was awaiting them beyond. I am sure they never grasped the full picture of what was to come. I saw them being beaten and whipped, I saw their solemn and desperate faces, their bodies squashed together in the confined space, shuffling along at the command of their oppressors. Many sobbing, some pleading, others going quietly. The ones who resisted were beaten and then taken to solitary confinement and starved to death; an agonisingly slow death. I stood motionless, in a semi-trance, watching the events of the past unfold. I witnessed the breaking of the human spirit and it was so painful, I started to cry. My wife cried and others were moved to tears.

The experience was profound and touched us all deeply. I could only imagine some of the atrocities the captives went through, I didn't think anyone could fully comprehend the full scope of this tragedy, the pain and the degradation of human life. The horror the captives were subjected to was unbearable. I still wonder how anyone could have subjected their fellow man to this inhumanity. When people ask why I'm not afraid of demons, I tell them I fear humans. They are worse.

After the tears came comfort and it was our tour guide who offered us consolation. She quietly reminded us that it was all in the past. I felt the fact that we had become aware of the history of slavery and having experienced some of the suffering was more than expected and truly valued. It was a humbling experience like no other and I felt privileged to be part of it.

We were next guided to centre courtyard where we were surrounded by various prisons. We were led upstairs to the first floor where a narrow staircase eventually led into the inside of a church. I was surprised to find myself inside a church directly on top of the dungeons below. A single floor separated 'heaven' from hell below. I looked at the guide and she almost smiled when I asked,

"So up here is where the captors, would come up to pray for salvation and forgiveness? What about the teachings of

Christ, to love our neighbour and fellow man? How could they even contemplate praying up here with all that was going on downstairs ... unbelievable!"

I was angry and quite vocal, I felt sick to my stomach.... What a blemish on Christianity and the essence and the teachings of Christ. I decided that my anger would not serve a purpose and we walked out of the church. It was the end of our tour and we headed towards the exit. Our amiable guide escorted us and was still recounting stories to me, she saw that I was much interested. I felt that she connected with me after I had described my visions. She never questioned me about the visions but accepted them graciously; this was Africa, where people were far more open and accepting of the paranormal. Outside, while waiting for our driver, we further conversed with our guide who enquired about our country of origin. I explained that we were Lebanese but had moved to London. I told her we had prisons in Lebanon that resembled the dungeons that we toured, overpacked and in horrible inhumane condition. I was impressed and touched by her reply.

"Let us pray that one day this evil leaves this planet and all of us in peace"

Ghana was a revelation to me and I learnt a lot from my first visit and more on subsequent visits but what will stay with me forever was the vision of the Portuguese soldiers and jailers battering the poor captives in that horrible room with a small gap from where they were pushed onto waiting ships. It affected me because I briefly felt the immense pain the captives went through. Although they were beaten into submission, shipped and enslaved, whatever was left of their souls stayed behind in Africa. Perhaps what kept them going was the hope that one day they would return.

I will never fully understand or experience what it must have felt like for the poor souls. I briefly visited the dungeon and experienced what I did, but I returned to the comfort of my home, my security and warmth far away from the pain. The image that will stay with me for the rest of my life is the small gap in the wall where sunlight poured in and one could view the beautiful ocean, a peek into paradise. Yet from that small gap humans were flung to be sold as commodity in the free world.

My visit to Al Mina Castle was a humbling experience like no other. The visions that I had during my visit gave me a taste of cruelty and how truly unjust our world is. I can never forget the faces of the poor captives, may their souls rest in peace.

MAURITIUS

My wife and I flew to Mauritius for a holiday. We always dreamt of going there but we had to save for it and wait for the opportunity to go.

After a long flight from London, we arrived at beautiful Mauritius and went to our resort. It was fantastic with so many features but most important were the massage treatments that they offered. I was never a fan of receiving massages mainly because I am ticklish but my wife insisted that I should try it, at least once. She booked me an appointment with one of the female therapists who appeared to be warm and friendly and promised that it will be a relaxing experience. The therapist and I chatted and she initiated me into the process and explained that the treatment had religious associations and that the person receiving the treatment is to be treated like a god.

The massage took place in a small hut with an open roof for light and was surrounded by nature's ambience. Before we went in, she asked me to remove my slippers and then she poured water from a small barrel on my feet and knelt in front of me and prayed. It was customary prior to treatment to pray, for the person's blessing and healing. I felt her prayer was genuine and not some form of acting to impress tourists. The small hut had a beautiful and soothing energy, I felt comfortable.

My wife had booked me a deep healing massage session that was to last a couple hours. The masseuse started the treatment and I quickly realised just how tense I was. Soon, I abandoned all thought and closed my eyes and started to drift far away. The feeling was so incredible and before I knew it, I saw an incredible vision of an Indian lady in a red sari with golden edges. She was smiling, wanting me to know that she was specifically communicating with me. She was young with black eyes and hair and light skin. I will never forget her smile, warm and affectionate, with a beautiful twinkle in her eyes. She showed me a small village and a tree, I saw little children and animals. I could not fully understand their significance, I was lost to the beautiful energy emanating from her, I knew that this was not an ordinary spirit but an evolved entity in human form. She communicated telepathically and her eyes were simply incredible, they were looking straight into my soul, as if they were gently caressing and comforting me. I never felt uneasy or uncomfortable at any time. When my treatment ended, it took the masseuse a little time to wake me up. The first thing that I said to her was 'I saw a vision' and she was intrigued. I could share my experience since I was in Mauritius, a spiritual and open country. She offered me herbal tea with honey and sat opposite and listened to my story. I told her about the lady that I saw, I described her and what she had said to me. The masseuse was quite excited and asked me all sorts of questions about the lady. She asked me if it was possible for me to wait while she fetched a friend, I felt a bit awkward but I agreed. She returned and they both listened intently as I recounted the vision that I had. They asked me to repeat the description of the lady a couple times, and then they started talking in hushed tones. I asked them if there was a problem and they said no, they said that what I had seen could be a blessing if indeed it was who they thought it was. My masseuse asked me if I knew anything about the Hindu religion and I apologised for my ignorance but I really knew next to nothing.

I was keen to return to my room, knowing my wife would be waiting for us to have lunch, so I excused myself. I walked to the reception and they followed me. They produced a small card with a drawing of a lady in a red sari at the front. It resembled the lady in my vision but the drawing did not do her justice, she looked more beautiful in my vision. I confirmed they were one and the same, and they were taken aback and expressed great joy. I was confused as I did not understand the significance of my vision but I could tell that to them at least it must have been important. They asked me to recount the vision again and they were clinging to every detail, especially my description of her, her hair, eyes, colour of her sari, the golden patterns and embroidery. I told them that she was warm and made me feel peaceful and yet something about her was different, she was no ordinary human. They agreed and smiled, they said that they recognised her as Lakshmi, the Hindu goddess of wealth, health, fortune and prosperity. I am ignorant of the Hindu religion so I did not know or appreciate the significance of it all. They kept repeating how blessed and privileged I was to have had this vision of her and that she is a Goddess of great importance in Hinduism. I was touched by the experience, I felt that it was a great honour.

Later that day, I recounted my experience to my wife and she was also deeply touched. She said that I should cherish this beautiful and most blessed experience. The next day, I craved going into cold water, despite detesting it. I dipped into the frigid sea and swam alone. I found it comforting and a great relief, it re-energized me and also helped me to settle down and become grounded again. I could not sleep the night before, a combination of a faulty air conditioner in our room an excitement from the day. I strolled around outside as my wife slept inside and I watched the stars in a clear sky, the cool breeze was welcome and helped me to eventually feel sleepy. It was hard to stop thinking of the vision and the lady's mesmerising eyes. I knew that there was something unique and special about her. There was also a sense of beautiful familiarity, a oneness ... it really felt amazing.

A few days later my wife organized a tour on a private speedboat to visit different attractions. Our guide doubled as the speed boat driver and he was friendly. It helped that we spoke to him in French as he was struggling to express himself in English. We set off from our small harbour and our driver pushed the speedboat to nearly top speed and we almost skidded over the water, he was quite enthusiastic to impress. He told us he needed to get us to one of the last stops as quickly as possible so that we could enjoy the rest of the tour before sunset.

He drove parallel to the shore and then veered off into what appeared to be a river. He dropped his speed and we slowly drove past rock formations and hanging trees, it was spectacular. My wife and I were absorbed in nature all around us, this was definitely worth the boat ride. The driver took the boat closer to the rocky river bank and my wife asked him if it was okay for us to get off the boat and look around and he said yes. Immediately, I felt a rush come over me, a powerful sensation that froze me. My wife waited for me to confirm I wanted to join her but I could not communicate. I felt detached from that reality and in my mind's eye, I saw her again; Lakshmi. It was the same beautiful and peaceful sensation I felt when I saw her in my vision but now, it was even more powerful. My wife asked me again, but I said, "There is a shrine in her honour behind the trees."

"Who? Where? I cannot see anything." Indeed, it was not visible from where we were moored, the riverbanks were dense with foliage.

"It is there.... I know it is there, I can feel it."

I asked the driver if there was a shrine for Lakshmi behind the trees and perhaps due to my poor French, he did not seem to understand and kept asking me to repeat myself. Eventually he understood and confirmed that indeed there was a shrine in her honour, but it wasn't visible from where we were. He said this was a spiritual area the locals frequented for contemplation and prayer.

I too surprised and deeply touched so I said a silent prayer before we continued on with our tour.

Mauritius was special for me, not only was I privileged with an incredible spiritual experience, I was also fascinated at how closely integrated were the Mauritians who are religiously diverse. I saw mosques, churches, Hindu temples, etc., side-by-side, often separated by a single wall. I asked my taxi driver if there were any sectarian issues between the different religions and he was surprised with my question. He immediately replied and said no, there was nothing of the sort and that they all lived as one large family. He was fascinated by my question and asked me to elaborate further on why I asked. I explained that in other parts of the world, unfortunately, discrimination was rampant and it is actually rare to learn of a society where harmony prevails. He was amused and told me that when they pray, they go into each other's places of worship. They celebrate all religious holidays together, interfaith marriages are common; they consider each other as part of a single family.

I have rarely if at all come across a balanced society such as the one in Mauritius. I was fascinated to learn how simple their lives were and how truly spiritual they all were. I learnt so much from the Mauritians and they did help restore my hope. Maybe one day, the rest of the world will learn to become civilised and follow in their footsteps.

I feel that I was perhaps being prepared at many different levels but of course, I was yet to discover the true purpose behind it all and in time all the pieces would fall together and form a complete picture. Mauritius was one significant piece of the puzzle. My psychic ability was being taken to new levels, I had an unforgettable experience and communion at a very personal level with a deity, one that is so sacred. I will forever cherish the memory and treasure the privilege that I was allowed because it gave me more hope.

The angels are watching....

PATIENT S. – BURNS VICTIM

I keep details on my healing service very private and do not publicly share that part of my life. I keep a very low profile on the subject for many reasons, mainly to avoid ridicule and also to limit fascination and needless conversation about the paranormal.

In the case of patient S., it was a unique experience and I learnt many lessons, including that people in general appreciate good intentions, even if they do not necessarily believe or accept what I stand for. They still value and appreciate my efforts and that I am trying to do something positive.

Patient S. was a local shopkeeper and I used to pass by her shop frequently. One day, it dawned on me that I had not seen her for a while09, so I casually enquired with one of her staff and was told that she had met a very serious fire accident at home and was a burns victim at a local hospital. Unfortunately, patient S.'s chances of survival were very bleak. I finished the conversation and started to make my way back home, but I just could not bring myself to leave, I felt that I had to say something about healing. It was very awkward because I had never spoken about such matters with S. or her family. But, I had to do what I felt was right at the time, regardless of how it would be perceived. This was a very important step forward because I summoned the courage to reveal myself to people who I see locally and quite regularly as a customer and even a friend.

"I am told that you have healing powers, that you can help my sister," S.'s sister said to me.

"I believe in prayer; I will try to do my best for her but that is only if I am invited to do so."

"Yes please ... if you can help in any way, please ... "

I was so relieved to have opened up and shared with her. She thanked me and later that day I joined her at the hospital to visit her sister. S. was in ICU (Intensive Care Unit). When I first saw her, I did not even recognise her. Her face was bloated and dark red in colour and she wasn't responsive. She was being very closely monitored by junior and senior doctors coming and going at short intervals. There were over twenty patients in ICU surrounding a middle island base where the doctors gathered. My concern was that I did not have privacy to go ahead with my healing. I felt awkward but at the same time I had to deliver what I was there for. I looked at patient S. and felt sad for her, she did not look well. She was gasping for breath occasionally and sometimes writhing as if in pain or discomfort. I closed my eyes and asked for guidance and once again, the immediate feeling was that I should pray. I was in ICU and under the watchful eyes of scientifically- minded people, doctors and nurses and I had to shut all of them off. I knelt by her bedside and made the sign of the cross and prayed, asking that I may be granted the privilege to serve. This is how I always start my healing service; I ask to be allowed to serve and then I surrender myself to the blessed warm light.

I stood up and caught a glimpse of the medical team. They were going about their business and none paid any attention to me, so I closed my eyes and held the patient's hand and started praying. It was hard for me to 'shut down' and to ignore my surroundings because I was very self-conscious. What made it harder was all the beeping and various alarms going off at random intervals. Doctors and nurses were speaking and dashing all over the place, sometimes, even showing up next to me to check on my patient. I had to step up to my task and forget about all that was going on around me. I was especially apprehensive about being in the heart of a gathering of 'scientific' people and was anxious about how I would be perceived as I was delivering my healing. I reminded myself of my purpose and that I was there for a good reason, I continued to pray. Soon, I started to faded and everything around me was became insignificant. I was no longer worried or anxious about anyone or anything, I surrendered myself in service and the beautiful warm healing sensation took over me. I ignored the patient's reactions or even the lack of them. I cleared my mind of all doubt and prayed, hoping that she'd be is given a chance. I pleaded that she be spared suffering and that she'd be healed. My prayer became a mantra and I found myself repeating it over and over and I just went with whatever my feelings were guiding me to do. Suddenly, I felt someone wiping my face, but there was no one in the room.

I remember that sometime later, I opened my eyes, glimpsed my surroundings. An angelic being, with wings and a very bright white, leaned over from the foot of the bed. The vision was no longer than a split second before it vanished, but it bore a lot of impact, I felt that healing was taking place and it gave me hope that the patient might make it.

At the end of the session, the patient's sister thanked me, and I asked her if she wanted me to return and she said yes.

I saw my patient a few more times, but she did not improve, which puzzled me. Other patients usually improved after the second session. In this case, there was nothing that assured me of her improvement, and I found myself at a loss after many visits. Something was wrong, and I wasn't helping her. Her sister thanked me for my efforts, and we agreed there was nothing more I could do. I had to consult with Paula.

Paula could see from my face that I was very upset and feeling down, she invited me in for a chat. I explained what had happened. She listened carefully and nodded to acknowledge every so often. I concluded with the fact that I was feeling that the whole affair had been a waste of time and that I should perhaps not have volunteered my help. I was confused because I saw that majestic vision and felt assured that the patient was in good hands.

"I do not understand what it was all about Paula, where has all that healing gone? I feel it was a waste of time! In fact, I feel stupid for going there all these times for nothing!"

"Healing never goes to waste, it will always find someone to whom it is intended."

"I cannot think of anyone more needy than Patient S. But she hasn't improved."

"Yes, I understand that this patient's condition has not improved, at least in appearance but healing never ever goes to waste. Healing will always finds its way to those who need it the most."

I took everything she was saying on board but I still felt a conflict within. I genuinely and very strongly wanted my patient to improve.

After a little pause, Paula went on.

"You cannot dictate any part of the healing process; you are just the instrument. I know that you want the best for your patient, but have you even considered the possibility that perhaps she is not meant to be healed?"

"If she isn't meant to be healed why was I there? What the hell was I doing there, putting up hopes?"

"You were there to support a family through a difficult time. I'm afraid that you do not get a say in who gets healed, you just serve and support whichever way you can. Look at the bright side Garo, you genuinely tried to help, gave her sister comfort and strength, which is more than enough that anyone can ask for at a desperate time of need."

"What about the vision that I had, I saw an angel for a fleeting second. What was all that about?"

"That was a beautiful experience which you must cherish. There are many possibilities behind your vision, you will eventually find out the reason behind it. Maybe it was God's way of giving you the determination to continue to serve. I do not know and do not want to speculate further but believe me, everything will come into place."

Months later, when I had put the whole experience behind me and sort of come to terms with the fact healing was beyond my control (I am a control freak by nature) along came the conclusion to this episode. I was on my way to the underground train station, rushing to a business appointment when I ran into S. and her sister. I stood there, baffled and shocked, at a loss for words.

"Hello Garo ... " Patient S. greeted me, she was using a cane for support, she looked frail but also quite strong in her own way. She had a small scar on her throat from a breathing tube. I was very emotional, happy and shocked to see her and delighted that she was alive.

S. hugged me and said,

"My sister told me that you used to come to pray for me at the hospital. Thank you, Garo." She hugged me again and I was lost for words.

I learnt a valuable lesson through that experience and that is never to give up. In later communication, my communicator conveyed to me, "You must be the light, the beacon of hope. The darker it gets the brighter you must shine. Keep your faith strong, son...."

I learnt that I had no say in the end result and nor in any part of the healing process. I was and still am an instrument. The only control that I should have is over myself, my fears, my anxiety and my over overzealous need to be successful every time. It is true that I am a healer but I am not God, nor do I have any power to influence a patient's fate. I learnt that prayer can indeed move mountains but I also learnt to accept God's will which always prevails.

The sisters and I parted company as very dear friends and we are still connected. They truly appreciate all that I did for them and patient S. has always been vocal about me going to hospital to pray for her. I was once in a Chinese restaurant and was told by the manager that S. had told them about her experience and mentioned what I had done for her. He patted my shoulder and shook my hand. I was deeply touched and began to understand the significance and the beauty of healing, the selflessness and the sacrifice. The ripples from that experience and all healing experiences continue. Love can only spread and illuminate the recesses of darkness and fear, love conquers all.

"You were right" I took Paula by surprise.

"I am sorry?" She flashed a naughty sarcastic smile.

"You told me ... healing never goes to waste and will find

its way to whoever needs it."

"What do you think you have learnt from that experience?"

"So many things but to begin with, I should never base judgement on what my eyes see."

"That would be very wise indeed."

"But then, how come things changed so dramatically? The last I saw of her was that she was still the same as she was when I first visited her and that is why I concluded that she is perhaps not meant to be healed."

"These things work in ways that we do no fully understand. The good thing in all of this is that your patient has come through and that you are valued for whatever help you gave."

Patient S. recovered back to her old self and is now back in business. I frequently see her when I pass by her shop and whenever I do, her eyes connect with mine and she smiles as if to say, we crossed the dark tunnel together, thank you.

REINCARNATION

I have never been a believer in reincarnation. I could never grasp its concept even when I accepted so many other aspects of life. Over the years, I learnt that nothing can be ruled out, even if I didn't believe in something, it didn't mean that it may not be true or did not exist.

In my twenties, I couldn't tolerate hearing Spanish being spoken! My wife thought it absurd that I should be so deeply affected and she tried to make sense of it but we both could not; I cringed every time I heard the language. I love all people from all cultures, I had no logical reason to react in this manner. It was just the way that I was, and my wife put it down to one of my oddities.

In my younger years, I used to have a recurring dream, fragmented but the theme was always the same. I was in a remote South American village among the natives who spoke Spanish. In my dreams, I seemed to understand them but never paid close attention to what was being said. The dreams were quite surreal, there was always a strange feeling that there was a war or a battle taking place. I was a soldier who was attached to my surroundings; the village was my home.

In one dream, I was in a barn climbing above hay to the upper deck. I was either wounded or exhausted, struggling to get away from someone. Two enemy soldiers rushed in searching for me and I was hiding, scared. I looked down at them once again at the same instant one of them lifted his head and saw me and said something and aimed his rifle at me, I froze. He said something to his friend and they both laughed. He then shouted at me in Spanish, I tried to quickly retreat and he fired. I was shot and everything went dark, I woke up startled. The dream was so real, it took me a few days to get over it. It never actually felt like a dream, it was real.

A few months passed before the second dream. Once again, I was in South America in a bus on a rugged road. In the back on the bus was a soldier, hunched forward as if sleeping and leaning on his rifle for support. He looked exhausted and was swaying from side-to-side as the bus swerved to avoid potholes. I got close to the soldier when he lifted his head and looked at me. I saw a scruffy young man, unshaved, haggard and tired. He looked as if he was not only tired of being in battle but also of life. His eyes looked sad and I felt his desperation. Something about his eyes felt strangely familiar, he wanted me to know something. Then I heard a voice say "this is you."

In a flash, I recognised myself in that soldier, I caught a glimpse of a warped reality but it made sense. Whenever I mentioned the dream to others, the general consensus would be that it was probably from my past life. It was strange because even though I felt a strong familiarity with that soldier, I still could not bring myself to believe in reincarnation.

Then the years passed and both dreams became distant memories.

In 2014, my wife and I were invited to a wedding at Playa Del Carmen in Mexico. She was excited about the wedding and our travel to Mexico but I felt the urge to decline the invitation. I heard so much bad publicity about Mexico and how dangerous it was, ignorantly, I assumed that the issues were spread through the country, I later learnt that the issues were mostly confined to Mexico City. I also was not entirely comfortable hearing Spanish being spoken. Upon some reflection, I did not rule out the possibility that this may be due to a previous incarnation in a Spanish country where I may have been killed but this presented a conflict because I still held firm to my beliefs; I did not believe in reincarnation. Whatever it was, this was no time to be negative about anything, we were due to attend a wedding of a special friend and I wanted to make sure that we were both enjoying it.

We arrived in Mexico and were taken to the resort. Contrary to my previous feelings and prejudices, I actually loved Mexico and specifically the resort where we stayed. Despite me not speaking Spanish, I warmed up to the staff and service providers and incredibly at times I found myself vaguely feeling some of their dialogue as opposed to understanding it. Mexicans are warm and fun-loving especially if one gets to know them and the effort to appreciate their culture. They are proud of their heritage and of their past and what I found quite remarkable is their openness and attitude.

On the day of the wedding, an incredible party was organized. There was an open bar, music, fire shows, acrobats, etc. The atmosphere was electric and no expense or thought was spared making it a special evening. We were meters away from the shore, dancing away to good music, the party and company were fantastic and although I am not usually a dancer, I found myself on the dance floor with Claudine. I paid a visit to the bar and enjoyed a shot of double vodkas, then danced and drank some more. Although I had consumed a large quantity of alcohol, I was not drunk but merry, in full control. My inhibitions disappeared, and I found myself on the dance floor with a handful of girls!

Eventually we had to retreat to our room and the waiters summoned a buggy to drive my wife and me to our cabin. We got in and I sat in the front next to the driver and my wife just behind me. The ride lasted a few minutes and I do not recall any part of it, except that we arrived at our destination and my wife was staring at me puzzled. I did not understand her issue and I assumed that she may have been upset with me for being out of character and dancing and drinking. I went to the dip pool to smoke a cigar and to enjoy the rest of the night watching the stars. It was a beautiful clear night and the atmosphere was electric, the energy unlike anything I had experienced before. I felt the incredible homey energy of the place and a warm feeling, I wanted to stay there forever.

"Are you okay?" Claudine asked as she emerged from the room.

"Yes, is something the matter?" Her face was starting to worry me.

"Do you remember what happened on the ride here?"

"No, not really ... why? What is wrong?"

"Garo, you were conversing with the driver in Spanish throughout the journey and it wasn't just the odd word or sentence. You were speaking fluent Spanish ... since when do you speak Spanish?"It felt like someone had slapped me and I was numbed, how could it be that I was speaking Spanish? I had no idea....

After my initial shock, I went back to enjoying my cigar and the stars.... I did not want to think about it, I had no idea what happened earlier but deep down I felt that it was due to something that I could not explain. The sense of familiarity, the homey feeling ... could it be that I had been here before? Is reincarnation real? I reflected on my dreams of the soldier and the sense I received that he was me. How could he be me, if that is true, then where was that soldier now?

I had so many questions and no answers. I retired to bed, surrendering to a deep and peaceful sleep.

We left Mexico with heavy hearts because we loved it so much. Inexplicably at the airport, I felt teary, a strange feeling, as if I was leaving home. Part of me did not want to leave.

Since my experience in Mexico, my attitude towards all things Spanish changed completely. I no longer feel disturbed when I hear Spanish being spoken and in fact I have come to love Spain and I visit there with my wife and daughter often. I now don't rule out reincarnation as a possibility, I concluded that I am a limited human being, I have no way in knowing the full picture of what possibilities are out there. Till this day, I cannot explain how I ended up speaking in Spanish on that night and during my visit to Mexico. I have resigned myself to the fact that it is something that I don't think I will ever be able to explain. Yet again, I experienced the phenomenal and impossible become possible. All the lessons being learnt about openness and accepting the world for what it is and not for what I wanted it to be.

INSIGHT INTO MY PERSONAL LIFE

Being in service means making a lot of sacrifices. I had to overcome personal issues and anything that may present an obstacle to the service. Old bad habits had to die, as well as some types of social activities. I had to learn to put my prejudices, fears and opinions to one side and not to judge patients, even if they made obvious mistakes that led them to seek my help. This was difficult, and I still struggle against my own imperfections and failings. I always remind myself that there is eternity ahead so that I do not become complacent or over confident; I can always do better.

The paranormal is a fascinating subject, the mystery that surrounds it draws many people to it and also scares others. Some go to extremes to learn about it to discover hidden 'truths'. In doing so, many lose sight of themselves. I intentionally lost interest in the glamorous and mysterious side to the paranormal because I did not want to be distracted from my mission. I accept that there are elements to life, that are beyond what we regard as 'normal' but that is part and parcel of life. As for seeking answers, I no longer have an interest in that either. I have no time for questions or answers, my focus and priority are to help my patients and to live a wholesome and happy life.

Sometimes at parties or social gatherings, the subject of the paranormal may be opened and in the past, I used to immediately participate and speak freely and confidently. I used to genuinely believe that I had the answers, how little did I know. I no longer participate in such discussions, I find a way out if I'm included. It is fascinating how we all talk for hours on about things we don't comprehend.

There are those who fear the paranormal and avoid related discussions, I fully understand their position and do not judge them. I don't fear the paranormal as much as man's ignorance, which is far more dangerous as far as I am concerned. The paranormal should be respected and should never be treated as a pastime or a means for entertainment. It is not a subject for fascination, nor is it to be used for selfish gain or personal agendas. Even though I am actively involved and in service as a healer and exorcist, I do not have the answers, nor do I have any special privileges or knowledge above or beyond anyone else. The only time I may receive answers is when it is relevant to the condition of my patients and that is strictly limited to when I am in service. At all other times, I struggle with daily life challenges just like everyone else. I have come to accept, not seek 'enlightenment' or try to make logical sense of any part of the paranormal. I prefer to live a simple life than spend an eternity looking for answers, the majority of which I'll never understand.

No matter how hard I try to separate my personal life from my life in service, I can never totally 'shut myself off'. It is nearly impossible to do so when you are sensitive, it is second nature that one learns to control to some degree, but it does also operate seemingly independent of us sometimes. When I am with family and friends, I stop myself from tuning in to them, but sometimes, I still feel things. At times, this can be awkward or problematic because I may pick up something about someone and react negatively to it and I am not the best at disguising or hiding my emotions. The darker sides to people, even if concealed behind charm or warm smiles can be the trickiest to deal with, especially if I feel the presence of an external influence. My life has been complicated because of this. My wife and I have had many differences over people, including members of our families. In time my wife learnt to trust my intuition but more importantly, I learnt to trust her intuition as well which in some ways dwarfs my gift. My wife trusted her heart and gave me chances against all odds and despite a lot of pain that I caused her. She believed in me and still does.

Claudine and I enjoy a deep friendship and it to grows as we both learn more about each other. She has taken bold steps and changed in many ways to help me and be at my side on my journey. She is aware that some of my work involves scary moments, so I do not discuss my services with her, and she prefers it that way.

I also learnt to respect my gifts and to value my communicators and helpers. As is the case in any relationship, trust and respect are fundamental. I value the blessed angels, they reciprocate and give me love in abundance. Ours is not a casual relationship, so I do not try to communicate with them for fun or as a pastime. I take our relationship seriously and I observe respect at all times, it is integral. On very rare occasions, on a lighter note, my communicator may respond to a patient with a smile and with an amiable comment such 'you humour us'.

My gifts never needed developing, it is me who had to learn to come to terms with them and to trust the blessed angels that despite all the scary things that I am witness to, I will not be harmed. This took a huge amount of trust from my part because I had been hurt so many times especially by those I trusted. I have so far never been let down and if that should ever happen then I know to accept the fact that it is I who failed myself, the angels would never fail me.

COMING OUT TO FAMILY AND FRIENDS

For most of my life I kept my healing service a secret from my family and the majority of my friends.

I especially felt nervous should my business contacts or professional associates ever find out, I feared ridicule and judgement. My background is in Information Technology and I own a portfolio of websites. I always felt it necessary to conform and to act in a logical and acceptable manner. It was especially awkward to be in the presence of friends or contacts who would demean God or the inexplicable side to life, the paranormal. Many times, I stayed quiet and avoided coming to defences because I felt that their minds were set in their ways and maybe one day they would come to their own conclusions.

As time went by, I felt I was going against my own constitution, trying to be a person I am not. I saw no wrong in what I do, I have helped hundreds of patients and their families. I needed to break away from the shackles that held me for so long. Those around me could choose what to make of it.

I could not hide forever because eventually I had to be of service to friends and family. I could not go on, silent and not help them when needed. It was a big decision, and one that meant that there was no way to turn back. I consulted with Paula and she encouraged me to be myself. She said that most people who valued me would come to understand, if not accept. They would still appreciate who I am and respect my intentions.

My communicator came through in a dream state and showed me a star which became brighter and brighter until the image was flooded with a bright white light. He said that this was truth, it shines and illuminates and that it cannot be denied or ignored.

I understood the symbolic meaning of that communication and that the time had come for me to share the truth with others. I started by posting on Facebook.

Over the past few weeks I have been contemplating whether to write this post or not. The time has now come for me to openly share a side to me that I have kept private for many years. Although we live in modern times and what was once controversial is now accepted as the norm, there are still many grey areas. Especially when it comes to matters relating to the 'paranormal'.

I was born with a gift, one that I have learnt to cherish and to share—the blessed gift of healing.

My gift does not make me special in any way, it is a gift that is beyond me in every way. It is a gift that has changed the course of my life and allowed me to discover true love in helping others.

For many years, I have been in service, silently rendering assistance whenever I am asked. I have visited patients in hospitals, hospices, homes, flats ... anywhere I am needed. I am honoured to have been of service to people of all races, religions and sexes. I have shared their pains, their tears and their joys as well as their fears and horrors and nightmares.

Two years ago, I was granted full access to a church in London to use for my healing service. Every Friday, we receive patients who require help and my team and I offer our service for free. We have dealt with difficult cases, including victims of rape, abuse, drugs, violence, depression, emotional and mental illness. Hopeless cases, the majority of whom have nearly given up or have even been turned away from the medical world. We have also helped clear darker issues such as those of black magic, spells and curses, etc.

Week after week, I have witnessed the progress of my patients and their miraculous recoveries. I thank God and his blessed angels for allowing me the privilege to serve.

In writing this public post, I am not seeking recognition or appreciation for myself. My desire is for word to spread about the healing service at the church and I welcome anyone who needs help to contact me via private message. Please share with your friends and loved ones.

Together we are light...."

I cannot believe how well my post was received and I was overwhelmed with the incredible feedback and messages of support. My business associates were exceptionally supportive and sent me complimentary messages. One day, I was enjoying a coffee with our family solicitor and at the end of our meeting he surprised me when before parting he shook my hand and said, "Very proud of what you are doing Garo ... well done!" I had, in fact, forgotten that he was my friend on Facebook.

Friends, family and even complete strangers were supportive. I did not face any criticism, ridicule or a single negative reaction. Perhaps part of the reason is because we now live in modern times where we are taught to embrace openness, towards other religions, belief, sexuality, race, etc. Even towards subjects that do not necessarily conform to our reason or logic. The other reason, I feel as Paula said, people appreciated my efforts regardless of whether they believed in what I believed in. They learnt that I am trying to do something good.

The overwhelming support that I received motivated me to do much more than ever before and to further dedicate my life in service. I felt liberated in every way, I was now myself and ready to do God's work. To be in service as a healer and an exorcist without petty embarrassment or fear. I accepted myself and those who mattered to me also accepted me.

A few weeks later, my communicator came through while I was resting.

"We only find our peace when we are in the service of others, son." He smiled.

A CASE OF DEEP POSSESSION

A lady, who had been referred to me by a church staff member, walked into the church. I was forewarned that she was in a bad way, but had no other details about her condition.

She sat down, then got up and went outside, then returned and this process was repeated a few times. She was agitated and restless, disoriented and on closer inspection she appeared angry. There was hardly any warmth in her when I said hello, her colour was pale—her eyes sharp and piercing with a blank stare. She appeared soulless and trying to restrain herself.

I invited her to start the session and opened up with a small prayer. Her eyes looked even more piercing than before and I felt a distinct air of hostility. I felt that this was not going to be an ordinary session; there was something terribly wrong with the poor woman and her energy felt tense and angry. In fact the atmosphere changed in the church and everyone there felt it.

To start the process, I placed the Bible against her forehead and started with the Lord's Prayer. No sooner had I started praying, when she let out a deep and loud grunt followed by screams. They turned into ferocious roars and she pushed against my hand with phenomenal force. I had to summon all my courage and strength to push her away. She lunged at me like a wild animal and her strength, fuelled by her anger, overwhelmed me. I was briefly worried because she was strong and vicious and the rage emanating from her in the form of animal-like howls and shrieks was petrifying. My hand trembled, I felt afraid but I had to fight whatever it was. At that instant, I remembered my communicator and when he told me that my faith should be stronger than a rock and I felt that I was regaining my confidence and strength. This was a battle I had no intention of losing, the poor woman had to be saved from that which was haunting her.

The entity unleashed a torrent of expletives in a distinct husky male voice. This was not a female trying to speak in a man's voice, this was an actual man's deep voice. The entity threatened to harm its host and ranted that it would never leave its host and it threatened to kill her. I showed no emotion but my arm ached from pushing back, so I asked an eighteen-year-old attendee for assistance. I asked her to position herself behind the patient and to grab her and keep her firmly in place. This is when the real battle began, and the entity issued even louder threats.

"I will never leave, we will never leave ... oh ... you have no idea who I am. You have no idea!"

"I don't care who you are. You are defeated, and you will leave in the name of our Lord..."

"She does not want us to leave...."

"If she did not want you to go, she wouldn't be here. She wants you to leave and you will leave!"

"There are more of us, you do not know ... you have no idea! We are more."

"Makes no difference to me. I know that you will leave, regardless of how many you are."

I am omitting all the expletives and the dark language used during the exchange that preceded the healing and exorcism. I do recall that not only her voice changed but also her facial features, her eyes were now looking straight at me full of malevolence and I avoided making eye contact.

The attack intensified and the entity started screaming and shouting while I commanded it to shut up. It made different sounds, non-human and dark, we were on course for a showdown and neither side was prepared to back down. The young volunteer assisting me also struggled to hold down this woman. I prayed and asked for help, ignoring the entity. I had to keep my focus and ensure that I was not swayed or influenced in any way so that I am not diverted from the task ahead. When the entity took the Lord's name in vain, I slammed the Bible to the side of the host's face and pushed down hard while I commanded it to shut up. Whenever I had the upper hand, the entity weakened briefly and then resumed where it left off. I used similar tactics it was using and reverse psychology, which worked for brief moments until it recovered and attacked again. I was afraid, as I had no idea how it would end. I am not sure what was my biggest fear at the time, I just felt it become stronger and in my head. I thought that perhaps I had taken on a challenge that was greater than I could handle. I drifted in thought and considered my options and what I should do. I even thought of seeking help from other gifted friends in the vicinity. In a flash, all the thoughts stopped and I came to my senses; there was no one else to seek help from, I was to deal with this situation on my own. I felt that I should save my energy to be able to maintain the upper hand in this battle, I suspected that the entity may have been trying to tire me by using diversionary tactics to distract me.

The session was intense but the entity was beginning to understand it was hopeless to go on, it knew it was losing the battle. There was strong resistance against the host, trying to keep her seated, the entity was restless and defiant, the process was never-ending and getting worse. Suddenly, I was inspired to pray for the entity and to ask for its forgiveness. I focused on my prayers, silently praying in Arabic. I asked God to forgive the entity for its sins and accept it in His domain. I applied holy oil to the host's forehead where I drew the sign of the cross and continued to pray loudly:

"Lord, please accept this being into your domain and forgive its sins. It shall surrender itself to you in Christ's name."

The entity felt that something was taking place and for once I could see the expression on the host's face change—

it was worried about what I was doing. A renewed threat was issued about killing its host and I interjected:

"You can no longer harm her"

"I can and I will...."

"You cannot harm her or anyone else. I have just anointed you with holy oil, I made the sign of the cross and I prayed that you are accepted as a Christian. You are now a Christian and you will behave in accordance to our Lord's teachings. I prayed that the Lord forgives you for your sin. Surrender now and you shall be received..."

.The look on the host's face instantly transformed into disbelief, pure shock and horror. The entity realized it was losing its powers or advantages over us. The host stared back wide-eyed in disbelief.

"Leave her now and surrender yourself to the light.... The angels await you and your sins will be forgiven. You have my word; everything will be forgiven."

The patient backed off and slumped forward slightly and sighed a long, "No."

There was a long loud howl, followed by a deep grunt. It sounded like a wounded animal as the host fell on the floor. My helpers were slightly concerned for her wellbeing but I assured them she was fine. The entity eventually abandoned the patient, defeated. The deep growls eventually turned to sobs as the patient slowly came to her senses. When she was more composed, I helped her back to her seat, she was weak and confused. She covered her face with the palm of her hands and sighed.

"What the hell just happened?" She was disoriented and visibly shaken. It was as if she had woken up from a deep stupor.

"You were under the influence of something sinister but it is gone now."

"Are you sure that it is gone?"

I assured her that it was the case. Her expression was completely different from when she first walked into the church. Gone was the hostile and bitter gaze, the anger and the spiteful grin. She was now a different person, a lady, composed and respectable. Her eyes were friendly and warm.

One of my team members gave her some water and tissues. She apologized for her conduct, we explained that no apology was necessary. We were all exhausted and shaken from this experience. I was concerned for the welfare of my team and in particular the young volunteer. The woman's screams had been so loud and intimidating, another patient locked herself in a room.

The air cleared and the patient regained her composure and shared her background with us. She said that some time ago she found herself drawn to a man who, on the surface, seemed ordinary but she felt something was not right. She was fascinated by a 'mysterious' side to him and was attracted to him, ignoring the fact that an inner voice kept telling her to stay away. She discovered he was involved in the occult but was unsure in what capacity and to what degree. She found it fascinating because she was also fascinated by the subject. Somehow, she became involved in a quasi-relationship between the man and his ex-wife. After that, things got bad for her. At the mention of the ex-wife, I immediately felt something was very wrong and there was far more to the ex-wife than what my patient revealed or knew. I felt the ex-wife was the source of my patient's problems.

We bid our patient farewell and I asked her to return the following Friday. It was time to bring our healing circle to a close. I thanked the young volunteer and she disclosed her mother had previously been a patient and visited me on a few occasions for healing. She saw a vast improvement in her mother and this motivated her to start her path of self-discovery and enlightenment. She wasn't drawn by the fascination in the paranormal but rather for the purpose of being in service to help others and to learn about prayer and God. She said that she wanted to help others the same way that her mother was helped so I welcomed her officially as a volunteer into our group 'Light of Light'. She was delighted and she continues to serve.

We concluded with a prayer. I asked the volunteers to put the events of the day behind them and to get some well-deserved rest.

The next Friday, the patient arrived on time and we continued where we left off. She appeared completely different from her initial visit—calm and gone were any signs of her ferocious anger. She was composed and in control. I began my prayers and then I placed the Holy Bible on her forehead to see if there would be any reaction but there wasn't. I took the opportunity to ask her about her past and to continue to tell us about what led her into the situation that she was in.

She felt physically ill after being with the man she had told us about. It started one day after being intimate with him and she felt a weird cramping and painful sensation in her lower abdomen. It was as if something was 'deposited' in her. She did not attribute the condition to her former partner at first, although she did sense that he may be the reason for her suffering. By Christmas, her condition had worsened physically, mentally and emotionally, she could not leave her bed and a visit to the bathroom became a struggle. Then the nightmares began, followed by episodes of waking to a shadowy presence in her room. She heard the shadow's voice in her head. She was sure this was not a form of depression, a visit to the doctor confirmed this. She sought help from a local church and after their initial examination, they dismissed her and told her there was nothing they could do for her. She felt that they were trying to rid themselves of her. Feeling hurt and betrayed, she became more desperate, so she contacted a Spiritualist church in London and she was referred to me.

"One night I woke up because I was being choked. I struggled against a hand pressing hard on my neck and then it dawned on me that it was my own hand and my arm.... And I had no control over either. Something was controlling me, and I could not stop it, I was terrified!"

When she recalled this experience, it was obvious she was absolutely terrorised by it. Unfortunately, as is the case with many patients who seek help, there is also an element of fascination in the paranormal that renders them vulnerable and I have consistently witnessed it and tried my best to make them understand the seriousness of it. I try to stop them from being fascinated by the subject. The paranormal is not an object of fascination. There is little that we know or understand about it. It operates at different realms and well beyond our comprehension and our limited five senses. It defies all logic, limiting scientific observation and even making it redundant. There is no specific pattern to it and cannot be dissected or understood using mainstream scientific methods. The entities on the other side have a far greater advantage over us because we are limited by comparison

The patient described how after her exorcism, she fell into deep sleep for a couple days. She finally found her peace and her body followed. I told her my feeling was that the ex-wife had a lot of influence and there was an element of punishing her, degrading her and maybe even a sexual obsession of some sort. The patient confirmed that she sensed that it was the case.

We prayed, I placed the Holy Bible on her forehead and this time, there were no hostile reactions. I smiled to her and she smiled back, she was clear. We all felt delighted to see her improve and to see her clear of that dark and sinister entity.

We recommended that she seek therapy to help her further, there was a lot more to clear within and it would be best conducted with the help of a professional.

The patient continues to visit me occasionally for regular updates and chats.

I sincerely hope that my book will enlighten others to steer away from the fascination in the paranormal so they can enjoy wholesome lives without losing themselves to that which is inexplicable. Developing mediumship, healing and psychic gifts is acceptable with the help of experienced and responsible persons. Activities for the purpose of thrill seeking such as Ouija boards, visiting haunted homes or communication with spirits or other entities by inexperienced individuals, pose a grave danger. These activities are quite common among the younger generations and thrill seekers who seem to be drawn by the mysterious side. I am not a psychologist, so I cannot comment on why the young seem to be drawn to this sort of thing. I hope one day preventative measures are put in place so that younger generations are taught about these subjects in a transparent manner to minimize the dangers involved.

Where there is a physical disturbance in a house such as a haunting, it signifies the presence of either an unhappy soul or souls or it could be due to something more sinister and possibly even evil. Whatever the reason for the disturbance, it is not cause for cheap thrills or entertainment. I fail to understand how people can find entertainment in the suffering of others or the logic behind 'ghost investigators' types of TV shows.

The hardest part is for parents or carers of the patients. They witness a strange and inexplicable transformation in the patient, along with serious physical, mental and emotional manifestations that eventually lead them to conclude that the person before them is no longer the person that they once knew. They accompany the patient to a doctor and the doctor usually prescribes sedatives and when these fail to deliver, the patient may be referred to a therapist or a psychiatrist. When no positive results are achieved, the family, if religious or believers, may consider a visit to a religious figure. Sometimes such a visit is successful and the entities are removed but in the majority of cases, prayer alone does not help. In my experience, an exorcist is one who is born with the gift and it takes a natural to confront the entities in a manner that forces them to abandon their hosts. I don't think this can be taught or trained for. Procedures may be followed, prayers may be repeated but the bottom line is that the exorcist has to be prepared to abandon all reason, all logic and fight back with a resolute and determined mind and allow the light to shine through him or her and into the patient to cleanse them. The light will only shine through the faithful who are pure of heart and gifted to do God's work.

SOME OF THE DIFFERENT TYPES OF ENTITIES

The most popular entities appear in human form. They reflect humanity on this side of the spectrum in that they appear as different colours, races, religions, etc. They share a common purpose: they seek human hosts to attach themselves to for many reasons—curiosity, parasitical, obsession with a person, possessiveness and sometimes even sexual fascination. Earthbound entities link with people who share similar traits. For instance an angry person may attract an angry energy, a gambler may attract an addiction. Some entities want to destroy their hosts. A strong sadistic element is involved here, perhaps the entities feel better about themselves seeing humans falling apart.

Some appear more experienced than others in operating stealthily to remain undetected for as long as possible. They keep their influence to a minimum to draw suspicion from the host or the host's family or friends. They are clever enough to even withdraw almost completely from the host if they are detected or investigated, only to return later and sometimes even stronger than before. There are times when entities claim a right to their attachment to a host citing the host's willingness or openness to the idea of 'linking' with some invisible force. They may even employ trickery to gain the host's trust, common deceptions such as appearing as someone else; a loved one who may have passed. Since the entities have complete disregard for their hosts' welfare and wellbeing and their presence is intrusive and serves no good purpose, I believe they are demonic manifestations. It is generally believed that we have guardian angels who watch over us but equally the dark side also do the same but for the purpose of breaking us. The more we despair, the weaker our faith and the more distant and resentful of God we become. This is what entities primarily want to achieve.

THE TRICKSTER

One case I dealt with was in fact a psychic medium who gives readings for a living. Her friend's husband passed and the friend asked the medium to link with him to give her messages. They had a sitting and sure enough the husband's energy joined them. Confirmation and proofs of survival were delivered, they were both pleased to hear from the husband once again.

A few days later, the medium awoke from a dream where the deceased husband communicated with her. He interrupted her sleep and she found that odd. She called her friend who asked her to keep the communication going. The medium told her that ordinarily she would not entertain this option but she'd make an exception. If she sensed him again, she'd invite him to communicate. A day or so later, while conducting a psychic reading, the medium felt the husband's energy in the room and she could not ignore him. She failed in her reading and had to apologise to her client as she found it impossible to stop thinking him. This intrusion became more common and she was stalked by this energy at public gatherings, during her group meditations and at the most unreasonable times. She could no longer shut him off and was starting to feel anxious. Her energies were at an all-time low.

Her sleep was dramatically interrupted, she woke at odd hours with an eerie feeling, as if someone or something had been in her room while she slept. This became so bad she eventually stopped sleeping most of the night.

When I first met her, she was so disturbed by events in her life, she was afraid and was almost whispering. She told me of this uninvited energy. I concluded her healing session with a prayer and wished her well. I told her to come back if she needed to. A couple months later she returned, looking even more desperate. She looked physically unwell, she was stressed and losing her hair. My initial assessment and gut instinct was that she was being taken over by the spirit she had previously described. I knew from past experience that spirits of loved ones do not inflict this sort of harm so I suspected we were dealing with a totally different energy and not her friend's husband.

We started the session with a prayer and as I let go of my thoughts and surrendered myself in service, I saw it; an entity and it was definitely not her friend's husband. It appeared as an Asian man, with a beard and a turban with a beaming smile but as always, the eyes gave him away. The smile turned to a grimace. It was enjoying the process: punishing the patient and challenging me at the same time. I ignored its communication and focused on projecting my energy onto the patient, surrounding her with a white light and the image of the crucifix. The entity tried to interrupt me a few times, by taking away from my focus. I pushed the mental image of it away and thought of it again. I realised it was trying to link to me the same way it had done with the medium, so I recited the Lord's Prayer, to help me stay focused and grounded.

It was a mental battle, and I felt tired and drained but I had to persevere. We were on a mission to get rid of this unwelcome energy and to help put a stop to a poisonous situation that was wrecking my patient's life. I kept visualising a bright white light surrounding my patient and intensifying in brightness by the minute. I felt the entity weaken and so I visualised a solid wall of white light surround my patient. I was then inspired not to focus on the process but to surrender myself to the calm to allow God's angels to do their work. The challenge for me was to shut off the energy in my mind, it was rambling on and on and was overwhelming me at times. I did feel that I was losing control of my mind, I just could not shut it off. I felt sad for my patient and understood what she must have been going through, it was hellish. Slowly I felt calmer, and the calmer I felt, the stronger I felt and the weaker the intrusion from the entity. When it was sufficiently subdued, I asked the blessed angels to take care of it while I focused on the patient who was oblivious to what I was going through. I calmed the patient and gave her strength and faith. I recounted some of my findings and told her that her life was now due for a change. This was the time for her to take bold steps moving forward and to have faith in God and his angels. As a start, she was to put her mediumship and any related activity on hold for a while. This included psychic readings which was a difficult step for her not only for financial reasons but also because it was her passion. I sealed the patient with a prayer and asked her to close down her psychic channels (chakras) at least twice a day. I also recommended that she research a specific supplement to help her find her calm to help her sleep again. The patient reported positive results and with the help of supplements and prayers she was on course to a full recovery and back to her health and life.

I did not fully grasp the reason behind this entity's intrusion into my patient's life, but I did feel that she was lonely and possibly depressed. I felt that she was connecting with the other side for all the wrong reasons such as pastime or curiosity. She did not reveal the full picture, but I did not need it either because my gut instinct told me that she was going through the process to learn a valuable lesson. I did not try to investigate why the entity felt drawn to her because I did not engage with it.

THE SNAKE AND THE FEATHERED ENTITY

During the clearance of attachments, I have come across either a serpent or a feathered bird-like creature. I do not know where these entities originate from or why they choose to attach themselves to specific hosts. I do know that they are parasitical, possessive of their hosts and are powerful. Sometimes they appear part-human but they are easily recognizable, I feel their energy regardless of their appearance. I am not sure why the shape shifting occurs and if it is intended to cause confusion or if these entities are actually part human to begin with. All I know is that their presence in the patients' lives is unwelcome and is distressing and damaging. Patients suffering from these entities show a serious lack of enthusiasm and a sense of worthlessness, many self-harm and even lean towards suicide. Although they hurt silently, it shows in their eyes, faces and demeanours ... usually gaunt, greyish and deflated. I have observed difficulty in communication when patients try to express themselves. They become agitated, anxious and nervous. Sometimes, there's incoherent babble that's difficult to follow as the patient appears not to grasp partial or whole sentences. I see fear and anger in their eyes. With prayer, trust and a good dose of love and humour, positive results are achieved. Patients with these types of attachments find it hard to connect with or trust anyone. They become isolated and detached from the real world. They need time to emerge from their 'hiding' and to reclaim themselves. It pains me to see them in such a state but I know that it is not for long. God's light will shine through and save them....

When I meet new patients, I study their behaviour and look for obvious characteristics or tell-tale signs of an external influence. Sometimes I see obvious physical effects of the attachments on hosts, other I sense their presence or I may even see them in my mind's eye. Although I do have an inquisitive mind I do not engage with the entities. They are there for a specific reason, not necessarily a good one. I encounter the serpent on more occasions than the feathered entity, it seems to be more common and especially prevalent in patients who are victims of black magic or other related practices. Patients suffering from these energies sometimes display visible and distinguished characteristics; they resonate a coldness and during treatment, they may struggle to communicate and become sluggish and physically challenged. This is a powerful entity that is to be reckoned with and not be underestimated. Its sole purpose is to destroy the core or the goodness of its victim and to render them an empty shell. Some of the nicest people I have met have suffered from the darkest entities and the snake energy has destroyed many lives and good people in consequence. I've witnessed this over many exorcisms.

The feathered entity does not communicate, but I have seen patients suffering with such a possession, squawk and choke as if trying to dislodge something from their throat. This entity presents itself in a dark, tall and winged form and the most distinguishable feature is that it appears to be faceless. I have visualised that it takes hold of its victims using its sharp claws and it tightens its grip. Interestingly, some patients have previously reported feeling a great weight on their shoulders and neck area, which is greatly relieved after exorcism and healing.

Shape shifters and tricksters are masters at confusion and deception and are mainly responsible for mental and emotional breakdowns. Shape shifters and tricksters have deceived the best mediums and healers and I also have been their victim. They appear as one thing and then change their appearance and characteristics. They enjoy the confusion they create and misleading a medium or a healer is a huge advantage for them. I was once working with a patient who was suffering terribly from cancer. She was quite prepared and had accepted her fate but she welcomed me as a healer alleviate her physical pain. I used to visit her at least twice a week and pray for her. One day, while I was starting to drift away as healing was about to commence, I saw a trusted figure in my mind and he was endearing and warm. He made me feel the was there to express how proud he was of my work and also give me assurance that the patient would be healed and fully recovered from cancer. I believed it, I had no reason not to and in fact it motivated me to do even more for the patient. Fortunately, I did not share this revelation with my patient but I am sure that she felt a renewed hope because of my enthusiasm. Her family was also inquisitive and wanted to find out what I felt was going to happen and I did hint to her husband that we were on course to a full recovery.

After some time, the patient did improve dramatically and the cancer totally vanished. The doctor, the surgeons, the patient and her family were overjoyed and I celebrated the news but I also allowed myself to be carried away and take pride in my achievement. During prayer and solitude, I saw the trusted figure on occasion and he congratulated me and made me feel that I was on top of the world. All went well for a while and I was engaged in other matters at the time when I heard the sad news that the patient was ill again, a new cancer had developed.

I was called back by the family and I stood there in shock trying to gather my feelings and thoughts as I saw the patient lying down looking ill and frail; death was near. I knelt beside her and prayed. Even though I wanted to do my best for her I did not lose myself in service as I normally did and I felt healing was not forthcoming. It was impossible to remove the image of the figure who had previously appeared to me. It was as if there was a connection of some sort to the present situation and I could not understand what it was. Unlike all previous sessions with this patient, I felt awkward and nervous to be there. I felt that I had failed her and her family.

I ended the session and was glad to leave the house. I felt shame and guilt and the two combined were devastating. Resentment grew in me and I felt this was the end of my service as a healer. The feelings and thoughts were suffocating, I was also desperate for answers, I had to see Paula; I needed clarity. We met and I recounted my experience to her and she listened intently. The fact that I was given the opportunity to vent my frustrations and anger, helped me tremendously. As usual, she spoke only when she felt it necessary to do so and by giving impartial advice.

"What you describe is a sad set of events and I feel that you have reached a level where you feel at odds with everything including spirit."

"Yes, I am upset that I was misled and in consequence, I volunteered information to the family that turned out to be wrong. I have been left with egg on my face and now I hate what I have done!"

"Don't be too hard on yourself, you need to go through

this process to learn. Every experience, good or bad, is a learning experience and this is an important one. I need you to take your time and to silently reflect over things. Think of all the good and bad things that you went through and everything that you now prefer to have done differently."

I thought long and hard and reflected on everything I could not think of anything specifically that I may have done wrong and I told her.

"What were you doing at the end of the sessions? Were you leaving immediately or were you staying to socialise?"

"Actually I would stay to enjoy a rest, coffee and the family's hospitality."

" ... and what's would you chat about?"

"General chats but we also would discuss the healing and some of my past experiences."

"I guess they would find some of your stories quite fascinating."

"Yes"

"Did it used to make you feel special or important to be in the limelight?"

"I would have to say yes."

"I understand ... "

She went quiet, I think it was her way to give me space to think things over. I already had an idea of where I went wrong,

"I was wrong to have engaged with them socially," I said

"I agree. You were there as a healer and not on a social visit. You should serve and leave and certainly never claim credit or enjoy the attention. You are just an instrument, that's all. You have to come to terms with your gift, Garo, otherwise you will fail yourself and others."

She was absolutely right, I felt important and special telling them my experiences and they were a keen audience. My weakness and shallow mindedness revealed just how truly unprepared I was for God's work. It was selfish of me to enjoy the attention and not focus on healing. As I spoke I saw myself sitting in the living room surrounded by an eager audience.

"It is your weakness, Garo, we've spoken about this before. I know it is hard for you to resist but you have to find a way, otherwise your service will come to an end."

"I understand what you're saying, and trust me, I will address this least desirable part of myself. However, I am perplexed why I was led to believe that the patient was on course for a full recovery only to discover later that she was not. Why did it happen, Paula? What was the purpose behind it?"

"It appears you may have been misled by the dark side. I see you are confused by what I am telling you but you have to understand that the dark side is far more powerful than you think. They can impersonate others, even your communicators and angels. You have to understand, Garo, that your gifts pave your path ahead in service of humanity and this does not suit the dark side who will try everything to stop you. What better way than introducing self-doubt and resentment? If you give up, then you would have fulfilled their desire in seeing your light put out and an end to a beautiful service that could benefit so many people, you cannot imagine to what extent."

I nodded in agreement. I didn't like it, but it was the truth it couldn't be faulted.

"The energy that communicated with you and gave you all false hope was intent on deceiving you. It misled you to believe that it was your communicator, but it was not."

"But it was him, it looked like him, felt like him and sounded like him!"

"The dark side is capable of many things, impersonating others is quite elementary for it. Now had you been more focused, you would've been in a better position to deal with the situation as opposed to being blinded. Unfortunately for the gift to work, you really need to be devoted in your service to God and to put a stop to your old ways. The gift does not make you special, it is not about you. It was given to you so that you may serve others and that is as far as it should ever go."

I fully understood and accepted what she said. Indeed in service, I have entertained the element of fascination but in doing so, I invited an undesirable element and pain to everyone including myself. I am sure this would have been elementary to some people but I was foolish enough to miss the obvious. It wasn't too long after I watched 'The Devil's Advocate' starring Al Pacino. The story is about the devil and his futile attempt at building up evil on earth by trying to recruit a sharp lawyer who never loses a case. After the devil's plan fails, we see the devil tempting the same lawyer back into sin by using flattery. The movie concludes with the devil saying, "Vanity is my favourite sin."

The words rang so true and made me realise that this is probably one of my weakest points that I really need to find a way to control. In a sense I am lucky at least to have identified this issue at an early stage but then I guess such is the case with everyone who ventures into the service of God; we all have to learn from our imperfections and faults. I am no longer ashamed of who I am and who I was, everything and everyone serves a purpose and we are all here to learn.

People often ask me, "Aren't you scared of these things that you deal with?"

I tell them that I'd be stupid if I wasn't scared. Some things are terrifying but nothing comes close to truly scaring me as much as my own failings. I have a responsibility to everyone round me, especially my patients, some of whom depend on me; healing is not a game or a pastime.

I now make sure to keep the foolish part of me to myself.

THE SHADOW

Years ago, I dreaded sleep at night and I always made sure to keep on a light. I felt I was being watched in the dark, by someone or something, a presence in my room that disturbed me and sometimes even scared me. Over time, my fear of the dark increased and I resented going to sleep, anxious about what awaited me when I was in bed. Sometimes, I felt the shadow was at the entrance to my bedroom or in the corner of the room. I dare look lest I actually saw it. I tried to ignore it, but I simply couldn't because I sensed it close by. Many a night, I got out of bed and spent the rest of the night in the living room, watching TV, reading or even sleeping on the couch. I hated being vulnerable, but I had no choice. Not only did I sense its presence but I also picked up on it being something dark and horrible.

This was in my early thirties and I did not possess the experience or the skills to deal with my fear or put a stop to this intrusion. I spent a long time afraid of the shadow which followed me even if I travelled abroad or if I slept anywhere else. There were times it was more intense and

I could not explain why. After some research, I discovered many people suffer from the same thing and most are too afraid to speak about it for fear of retribution by the entity or ridicule by others.

Over time, it became worse. The 'shadow' was no longer confined to the corner or entrance of my room. It was becoming more intrusive and drawing nearer to me. Although invisible, sometimes I felt its presence inches away from me. It felt like someone was staring at me. I was too scared to open my eyes and pray for it to go away. Prayer never helped, I nearly always ended up leaving my bedroom. On rare occasions, when I did not feel the presence, I enjoyed a restful sleep but these were rare. Sometimes I felt so anxious, I ignored my need for sleep. I was exhausted, but at least when I was awake, there was no shadow.

It was getting worse and one morning I woke up out of breath. I knew that it was there, hovering above me. I decided enough was enough, I was not going to leave my bed and run. I wasn't thinking as I ordinarily did, I just wanted to put a stop to this thing. The tension was incredible, but it was a battle of wits and I was not going to back down; I was angry and pushed too far. I focused and saw the entity in my mind's eye and heard its voice in my head; it was threatening me. I raised my voice and replied, "Come on! Get on with it ... do you think you can scare me? I've had enough of you!"

I remember shouting loudly. Not out of fear, but anger and I felt that if I came face-to-face with whatever it was, I would not spare it a good punch or two. There is a limit to my patience, and I refuse to be pushed beyond it.

"Go on then, if you want to do something then do it or else leave me alone!"

It felt great to get that off my chest, I felt empowered for a change; enough was enough!

I don't know what happened exactly but standing my ground worked. The shadow left. I managed to stopped the cycle. It has been many years since my sleep was disturbed in that manner and I have never felt that presence again anywhere around me. It seems that yet again, I had to have a taste of what many of my patients go through so that I can relate to them. In view of the horrors some of the unfortunate souls go through, I no longer take my wellbeing for granted; I am very lucky.

GOOD VS. EVIL

There are many schools of thought, philosophies and opinions about the 'other world'. Some spiritualists do not believe in evil spirits, demons or entities. They believe there are 'mischievous' spirits on the other side who get up to naughtiness on this plane. I do not share their opinion because they say the world of spirit reflects our world here on Earth. If this is the case, then the spirit world should reflect all of life's beauty and ugliness.

Some people think patients who suffer from attachments or possessions, may have mental, emotional or physical issues and this may be true in some cases. I have, in fact, come across such cases myself on a number of occasions and usually bring the session to an end and recommend therapy and a full medical examination for the patient. Some of them accept it while others don't since they are convinced that there is an external influence in their lives. Unfortunately, I am limited in what I can do to help in such instances and I do insist that they seek specialist help.

An Asian patient who barely spoke English spoke about an 'intrusion' of some sort from an 'evil spirit'. She was adamant that something was controlling her and taking over her and we struggled to understand what she was saying at first. As always, I opened with a prayer and then placed the Holy Bible on her forehead and she reacted. She grimaced and pulled her head back, then she swayed her neck and let out some noises while shaking. She appeared to be under the influence of something so I continued to recite my prayers even louder, more determined to help her by exorcising whatever was making her react in that manner. With the language barrier, it was difficult to communicate with her at the end of the session to determine a history or a pattern to her ailment. We tried our best but we ended up going in circles. I asked her to return the following week, hoping we would be inspired on what to do in the interim.

On her arrival for her second session, she displayed similar symptoms, glazed eyes and she just stared ahead almost past me. We proceeded with the session and again I held the Holy Bible to her forehead and made the sign of the cross on her forehead with holy water. The reaction was the same as the previous week. She writhed and squirmed, sometimes grunting in a low voice. I tried everything to bring her comfort by releasing what was affecting her. At the end of the session she appeared to respond and collapsed into a chair. I had other patients to attend to so I bid her farewell and asked her to call me to let me know how she was. It was still hard to communicate and I hoped she understood me. A couple weeks went by before she called again. She kept repeating 'not good, I, not good ... ' I asked her to come to church. I then remembered that I would be at church at a later time so I called her straight back. She answered in a normal voice and did not sound distressed as she did on the earlier call. Her accent seemed improved as well, I was surprised, I thought I had called the wrong number. So I greeted her by name and she asked who I was and I told her that it was me, Garo. Almost immediately, her voice became distressed and her accent turned thick again. I explained that we'd be starting later than usual that Friday and after I hung up the phone, I wondered what was happening. How come her condition and her voice changed in between calls. I sat quietly to reflect on the situation and felt that something was indeed not right about the whole thing and I no longer believed that she was necessarily affected by an entity.

The patient returned to the church on the following Friday and arrived looking dazed. She sat at the back and my team and I observed her looking up to the ceiling and she appeared to be talking to herself. I called her to the front and I had a brief conversation with her. She complained that she was unwell and that she was feeling 'bad energy' again.

I raised the Holy Bible to her forehead and this time, I just pretended to pray in Arabic while in fact I just repeated gibberish nonsense in Arabic and I included the names of a few obscure dishes for good measure. She began her usual reaction, rolling her eyes and shaking her head from side-to-side, she looked distressed and my fellow volunteers expressed concern. There was no reason for her to be reacting in that manner, after all, no part of that exorcism process was real. I felt that she was just performing and that it was all about attention seeking. The time came for me to put an end to this charade so I told her that there was nothing else that I could do for her and apologised. I asked her to seek medical assistance from her doctor. She told me that her doctor had in fact prescribed anti-depressants but they didn't seem to help. I stressed that she should see her doctor again and explain to him that she needed more help and that he should refer her to a professional. I could see that she may have well received this same advice previously and it was not what she was seeking. She left the church still in character, complaining about the 'phantom menace'.

I am not sure why her character and voice changed when I called her whether she was seeking attention or if she was indeed mentally or psychologically disturbed. I felt sorry for not being able to help her further but there was little that could be done to help her given that she was not suffering from a condition that I could address. In my experience I have sadly come across many such poor souls who are desperate for help. A few understand that their situation warrants specialist help and thank me before leaving.

LOVE, HATE
AND THREATS

Walking home from a heavy day at church, a young man in his twenties passed me and I did not give him second thought until he started yelling at me.

"You, yes ... You! Don't think I don't know what you're doing." He nodded with a grimace and walked backwards while saying,

"I'll get you ... you'll see ... oh yeah ... you'll see"

I stood my ground, motionless and expressionless. I wasn't afraid but I was at a disadvantage having come from a long day of healing at the church. A car approached and he was forced to the other side of the road. I would be a fool if I were to say that I wasn't anxious. London has a high level of stabbings and thugs roaming the streets. Motivated and influenced by drugs, drink or darker forces, who knows what he would have been capable of.

It was a valuable experience as it was the first time I was

approached by a complete stranger who delivered a direct threat. I wasn't as worried about his threats about 'getting me' as opposed to the fact that he said, "Don't think I don't know what you're doing...."

As an exorcist I've learnt not to underestimate any situation. Whether he was drunk, high on drugs, or influenced by something to make these threats, it made me think that I should warn my team to be vigilant.

On the following Friday, without recounting the event to my team, I updated them on the nature of our work together, I told them that it may be unsafe at times. I explained I had gone through numerous difficulties and somewhat dangerous experiences and I gave them a choice to reconsider their involvement. What fascinated me is that all acknowledged what I said and told me they did not care. They wanted to continue the good work and would always by my side. I was moved by their response and in a way, I thought perhaps they were being slightly naïve. I don't consider the pitfalls in my service otherwise I too should be thinking twice about it.

I love my team dearly, they are true angels

Some of the most hurtful attacks have occurred from loved ones, many who remain oblivious of their actions. My closest companions have unexpectedly turned against me and launched scathing attacks that hurt me badly. I was once having an argument with a family member and she shouted, 'I hate you.... I hate you!' repeatedly and for no reason. The argument did not warrant this sort of response, it was un-proportional and took me by surprise. The next day she apologised and was at a loss as to why she felt these strong negative emotions towards me. There was no justification. She cried and apologised several times, I calmed her down and told her that all was forgotten but the fact was that she had hurt me too much, I was ill throughout the next day.

Another family member verbally attacked me. I did my best to defend myself and I felt yet again I was being picked on because of my commitment to God's work. I hurt for a few days but I was also helped by a dear friend who over dinner told me to expect to be attacked in such a manner and that the attacks would occur from those who I love because they hurt the most. She reminded me that the entities are probably frustrated from failing to hurt me at the church and this was a perfect opportunity for them to inflict good damage on me and on others around me.

Luckily, I am surrounded by loved ones who are absolute gems at heart, and they have on all occasions apologised for their actions. I am always reminded to look past the attacks from loved ones. Otherwise I would continue to harbour bitter resentment and that is not fair, it would ruin everything, including the healing gift and my love for them.

On a darker level, however, I've had to deal with far more serious attacks that I was fortunate to thwart or be saved from somehow. I once was on a bus in London with my baby daughter. I was standing, looking over my daughter and I must have been day dreaming because I did not realize that the bus had come to a stop. I was staring out of the window when someone shouted, "Are you looking for a fight mate?"

Although he was a huge and muscular guy, I wasn't afraid. I struggled to understand what he wanted. My first instinct was that this was yet another retaliatory attack due to my healing service. When I did not move quickly enough for him, he roared loudly at me to get out of his way.

His voice stunned everyone on the bus and my daughter started crying. I had to control myself and not say anything or react in any provocative manner. I moved swiftly and gave him room to pass, then I sat down to comfort my daughter. I must say that his loud scream stunned and disturbed me, it was the equivalent of a hard slap to the face and in hindsight, I should have reported it to the police as verbal assault. I looked at my daughter, crying, a tiny baby and I felt terrible. At that instance, I hoped to God that she did not inherit my gifts so that she never endure what I went through. Overwhelmed with emotion, I found myself wiping tears from eyes and several passengers came and offered their support. Little did they know the real reason for my upset.

"When you serve God, you suffer silently...." was the message I later received.

Confrontations have been numerous, originating mostly from all types of individuals, some known or even unknown. When I detect hostility or anger, I learnt to avoid such individuals so as to not exasperate the situation any further. This goes against my nature because I can be confrontational and bitter at times but I have learnt to step aside and not to take things personally. I represent that which provokes them and what the entities resent or hate, I have to expect such a reaction every now and then.

One of my worst experiences was from my school days in England. I was shopping when two young men came into the store.

I glanced at them quickly but then one of them caught my attention, there was something inexplicable about him that made me freeze and I drifted away in thought. A strange feeling overcame me, I sensed something about him, something dangerous. I felt he had done something bad but at the time I lacked my present knowledge and experience to be able to tune in to determine what it was. I was paralysed, I could not move from my spot, nor could I shift my gaze. I felt the same fear that I imagine anyone would feel if they were to stumble across a dangerous predator. This was my first taste of fear, not as much of the person but of the feelings I was perceiving. The two saw that I was looking at them and they stared back, still, I could not move away, even though I saw their facial expressions change and they were no longer smiling to each other, they were now angry. In a flash, the one who I was focusing on, produced a flick knife and opened it. I remember looking at the blade and seeing the light from the inside the shop reflect briefly from its surface; it was long and sharp. We stood in silence just staring at each other. My fear began to rise and I had no idea what to do. The look on his face turned to pure menace and I felt I was in imminent danger. Why had I provoked such a situation in the first place I wondered? Why did I stare at them? I felt stupid and vulnerable but I could not find any words to justify my actions or to turn the situation around because I was gripped by fear. Then one of my friends stepped in and saved me by telling them both that I meant no harm and that I was 'not normal' and on medication.

The guy flicked down his knife and put it away. We walked in the opposite direction, my friend had his arm around me to escort me out of the shop in a gesture to make it appear that I needed to be helped. When we cleared some distance, we ran toward the coach waiting to take us home. Once inside the coach, the conversation steered to the experience that I just had and many students found it bizarre and laughed. The friend who 'saved' me enjoyed a laugh as well but not in a nasty way, I was grateful that he came to my help. I could not see the funny side to it, I was just lucky to have walked away alive and not stabbed or injured in any way.

That was an extreme situation and a close rub with the nastier side to life. Since then, I have come across many dangerous individuals and situations but now I understand my senses far better and can interpret my perception and situations clearer and when I feel that I should just keep a low profile and move on, I do just that. The dark side is far more cunning and should never be under-estimated, its force is immensely destructive and supported by large numbers of abiding servants on earth.

I feel that I must also recount an event that took place many years ago when Claudine and I were guests at a friend's home. Our host had invited other friends to dinner: a couple and a single lady. The couple seemed introverted at first and kept to themselves. We tried to engage but found them dry so we just enjoyed the get together and a good chat with the woman. There were drinks on the table and we helped ourselves. Our host asked me quietly if we were having a good time. He was slightly concerned because he thought the other guests, specifically the man, may have become off putting. I assured him we were having a good time. His concern was in place because his guest was starting to behave in a slightly rude manner. I thought it best to ignore him and just enjoy the social setting and the company of my wife and others.

Eventually, our host excused himself and retired for the night. He called me to one side and asked me to keep an eye on things and to call him if I needed anything. My wife eventually left so I was left with Mr. Pompous and the women. Mr. Pompous, got louder as the evening progressed, he poured himself a few drinks and his partner tried to stop him but he wouldn't listen. A couple hours later, he was drunk and obnoxious, talking over everyone, and then banging his glass on the table to interrupt us. It was childish and bizarre but we paid him no attention and the three of us continued our chat. His partner was becoming nervous and I felt the mood take a dark turn. I did not like this man, nor did I want to be in his presence but my host had asked me to stay until everyone left.

Mr. Pompous felt ignored and he did not like that, he turned to the single woman. As she spoke, he gave her a couple of 'gentle' smacks on her face and mouth, to shut her up. She raged at him and warned him not to touch her again. She was strong and could defend herself easily but I was ready to come to her rescue if she needed me to.

One way or another, he became aware of what I said to her even though I had tried to be as discreet as possible. He turned his attention to me and started provoking me, calling me different names, I ignored him and just smiled. When he started insulting me in a specific and direct manner I wondered if he knew me from somewhere. He said things about me that he could not possibly have known and this took me by surprise. I stopped smiling and he loved it and roared with laughter, satisfied that he had finally touched a nerve. I don't imagine he knew the real reason behind my hesitation but he took it as a sign of victory and reached across the table and gave me a couple of demeaning slaps on my face, I did not react. At the time, I did not know why I froze but now I know that I can go into a mental 'zone' knowingly or even unknowingly. In that state of numbness I usually start feeling things, specifically if the situation is becoming dangerous. The man carried on saying things but I was not paying attention. I was trying to make sense of my own perception and still wondering how he knew things about me. I used to believe only good people are blessed with God's gifts and for some reason, I wrongly assumed that people from opposite sides of the spectrum may be gifted in their own ways and not everyone may be using their gifts for a good purpose.

It was his demeanour that affected me the most because of the way he addressed me, his eyes staring into mine, while shaking his head as if to say that he knew me and knew me well. The sense of familiarity was eerie. Then came a new bout of fresh insults and I snapped out of my 'zone' in time to see he was going to slap me again.

I was going through martial arts training and had become fanatical about it. I wouldn't classify myself anywhere near to a professional of course, I was being trained to fight, minus the philosophy and I was being pushed to new limits every week.

I met his hand and grabbed his wrist and I twisted so that he was locked in pain. The women shrieked because of my sudden move. He was shocked and tried to pull back but I grabbed him firmly and kept him in place and added more pressure. He swore at me and tried to laugh it off, but it was all pretence, he was in pain.

"Are you going to shut up or what?"

He waffled on and I took no notice, at least he wasn't swearing at me anymore.

Just then, his partner spoke to me and asked me politely to let him go.

"My first impression of you today was that you are a gentleman, please do not let that go ... not for him."

I saw sadness in her eyes, I felt that this brute had been bullying her and hurting her. I was tempted to hurt him even more but I stopped because of her. He pulled his arm back and I could see that the experience had deflated him. He started waffling again and among some of the things that he was saying were physical threats so the other woman interjected and said that it was time that they left.

As the couple was leaving, the man turned round and tried to slap me again. This time, I lost my control and kicked him. He tumbled down a couple stairs and on the floor. His partner fussed over him as he tried to sit up. The kick was quite powerful and he was hurting. At the time, I felt empowered and felt satisfied but in hindsight, I know it was a lesson for me on what not to do in the future. It was fear that drove me above all else because he did indeed present an advantage when he read me psychically. It was unexpected and intimidating, I guess it made me feel vulnerable.

I recounted the events to my host the next day and told him I was embarrassed by my behaviour. He laughed it off and told me that it was about time that arrogant man was put in his place.

It was a valuable lesson, one that showed me my weaknesses and my strengths. Little did I know back then that the entities that I would be confronting twenty years later would make this pitiful man look tame. The worst was yet to come, and I learnt to pick my battles.

THE HEALING PROCESS

Every week we see familiar patients faces as well as new ones in the church. Patients are referred to me via word of mouth, some enquire via the church, others may be referred by other mediums and healers. In the majority of cases, patients are accompanied by their loved ones, family or friends. They arrive in the hope that their ailments or conditions are cured, and they patiently await their turn. Sometimes, as I observe patients, I notice that those accompanying them may need help and so I recommend healing for them also.

Patients are called forward when I am guided to them and my team and I briefly explain to them what to expect. It is during this time that I start to sense vital clues about the patient's condition and I open up with a prayer. I shut myself off and isolate my thoughts, I consciously put myself into a state where my thoughts are frozen, almost like daydreaming but without the visuals or sound. The images, the feelings and the sounds start coming through and I am given the initial clues to confirm with the patient. This helps me to establish a link with the patient and to assure them. The patient is unaware that their reactions are being gauged by the helpers on the other side. Healing is only received by those who are willing to receive it. Depending on the patient's feedback, I am guided further, and the healing commences if they are meant to receive it.

Every case is different, and the healing is never the same on two patients. There may be similarities, but it is nonetheless unique to the individual. The start of the healing is difficult because I have to be in a frame of mind where reality around me is shut off as best as possible. If I find myself drifting in thoughts and analysing, I ask for help from the blessed angels and I command my mind into silence so that I can be sure of the purity of that which is to be received. When the healing begins, a bond is slowly formed with the patient and I find myself linking with the patient very closely. I see images of their lives, their families, their loved ones. I see the good memories as well as the bad ones. Over time, a bond is inevitably formed between the patient and me, we share their difficulties. Sometimes when I feel that I have taken more than I can handle on board, I excuse myself and go outside for fresh air and sit quietly by myself until I feel well enough to resume my service. We smile, we cry, and we laugh together, the link with the patient, extends to include members of my team who I sometimes see from the corner of my eye, wiping away tears or rejoicing with a big smile when a positive step is achieved. There is a school of thought that a healer should not be emotionally involved with the patient but I don't follow protocol. I just follow my heart and so far it has not failed me.

Eventually when a patient shows significant improvement

and is ready to return to their lives, I feel the energy subside and I see the patient with clarity, the healing then comes to an end. I inform the patient that the time has come for us to part, but I also tell them to feel free to visit in the future. Most patients are sad to leave, they find it hard to part from the beautiful healing energy and the team. This is the hardest part of the healing for me, to bid farewell to those who I have become close to, but I am reminded that the link we shared will remain forever and there will be many more patients to come.

DAYS AHEAD...

I often wonder where my journey will ultimately lead me and for how long I will be able to carry on with my service. It is a race against time to achieve as much as I can while I am still in control of my faculties. Some of the aspects of my service such as exorcism or the clearance of curses, spells or hauntings require absolute control and focus. I have to be in good health and with a clear mind to function in that capacity.

Sometimes I wonder how long I can go on fighting temptation at so many levels while restraining my own inner demons and fears. The path ahead never gets easier but somehow it does become possible with faith.

Every week I meet old patients and new ones, and all are suffering in their own ways and for a multitude of reasons. Many of them suffer due to other people's actions. It pains me to see how cruel humans can be towards one another, and it seems to be on the rise, unfortunately.

My team and I hurt deeply after dealing with victims of abuse but we support each other and push forward with our mission. I have thought of giving up a few times, but I cannot possibly abandon those in need.

One day, I arrived at the church for my weekly healing service. I was under a lot of personal pressure and I struggled to go to church, but I did. After my opening prayers, I looked across from me and saw many patients sitting quietly, waiting for their turn. A quick glance reminded me why every patient was there. I remembered my communicator's wise words.

"You must represent light; you are their hope."

Seeing the faces of my patients, their eyes and smiles, reminded me I was doing the right thing and helping others. Despite it being a difficult day for me on a personal level, one of the best healing sessions took place and the church was filled with a beautiful warm energy of love. After seeing how the patient benefited, I felt a great joy. I was the one who was healed the most that day.

Many aspects of life remain inexplicable and the paranormal is perhaps a science in its own right that warrants more study and research. I doubt if any of us will ever become evolved enough to fully comprehend the paranormal. I cannot say that I believe in everything as there is a lot of questionable activity out there. Unfortunately, many people profit at the expense of others and this field does indeed attract opportunists as well. There is also a darker side attributed to the paranormal, which is sometimes exploited by unscrupulous characters for darker intentions. The consequences are that some people end up labelling all healers, mediums or exorcists as charlatans which is not the case. As in everything, the minority few, spoil it for the majority.

In time I eventually lost interest in searching for answers and accepted the 'mysterious' side to life as the norm. I believe that life is boundless and the possibilities are endless. It is us humans who are vastly limited by comparison but we have yet to accept that fact and if we do one day, then we would have truly embraced life, the universe and God.

There is a side to life that is inexplicable and defies all logic. I am witness to the undeniable truth. I am witness to the Light, the Light of truth, love and Spirit. The Light of Light.

THE END

APPENDIX

THE ENTITIES

I often get asked by my patients, Who or what are these entities? What is their origin and what do they actually want from us?

I do not know what the entities are or where they originate. I don't usually engage with them because they are intruders and their malevolent intentions are clear in their victims. Their presence in patients' lives is intrusive and destructive, they are opportunistic. It appears that they operate independently of one another but at core they serve the same purpose. They prey on the helpless and the impressionable, the weak in faith and the strong in hate and anger. They derive great satisfaction from reducing us, hurting us and breaking us. The majority of these entities employ trickery to deceive their hosts or people around them so they can remain undetected for as long as possible. Some are skilled in physical phenomena and will do anything, including physical manifestations to try and scare us or distract us. Most of the hosts are usually unaware that they have been intruded upon by such an entity and those around them may attribute changes in the host's moods or behaviour to a variety of reasons including psychiatric or psychological disturbance. The last thing that may go through their minds is that the host's condition is due to an attachment or possession.

The longer the host is subjected to an attachment, the harder it becomes to separate them to eliminate the problem. Some hosts will not cooperate and let go of the intrusion despite being informed of the consequences. They are usually fearful of retribution or they may be deeply intertwined with the attachment and do not feel that there is anything wrong. Many hosts report feeling down and empty after a successful exorcism. I explain that this is to be expected because they are now moving on with their lives minus the intrusive energy. Patients often feel something is missing from their lives, which is true to an extent but it's a good thing and they eventually see it.

With regards to the motive behind the entities' intrusion into our lives, my opinion is that since I have not seen anything positive or of value then I am inclined to believe that they are bad and sometimes downright evil. Unfortunately due to the nature of my healing and exorcism, I do not engage with the entities to find out more about them as most of what they divulge are lies. I am personally intrigued to discover their origin, but I keep my curiosity to myself. The entities know very well that they are playing a destructive role in our lives and sometimes I wonder if they are part of a larger scheme or if they are acting independently., Are they receiving orders and if so whose orders are they acting on? The answer may be simpler, if I were to attribute the entities' behaviour to the devil's bidding, for instance. I do know that in the last few years, there has been a noticeable rise in sufferers from such intrusions. This was confirmed to me by fellow healers and mediums who operate independently of me, we are seeing a significant rise in such cases. Some of them are becoming physical and dangerous as recently reported to me by a patient who whispered to me that she is being raped and physically assaulted nearly every day in her bed by 'shadow figures'. Her hands trembled in fear when she revealed this to me.... I believed her.

PORTALS

I am not technically versed on many aspects of the paranormal and I usually try to steer away from theories because most of them are based on personal opinions. I have learnt to accept the paranormal for what it is and I generally go with my gut instincts and, of course, the guidance of my helpers on how to handle matters. I am by nature inquisitive and can easily become fascinated trying to analyse deeper but when it comes to the paranormal, I have learnt to shut the side of me that tries to make sense of something that is far greater than I can possibly comprehend and to just get on with the task I have been assigned with.

In my service, I have come across portals on a number of occasions. Portals, as I understand them, are 'openings' or doorways into other dimensions. They may come to exist naturally or they may be opened intentionally or carelessly for whatever reason such as the result of tampering with the occult. It is also possible for portals to come about as a result of rituals or magic spells and curses. From what I have gathered so far, portals are a 'rip' between two dimensions or two or more realities. When a portal is opened, it can allow access to all sorts of uninvited energies into our world and these energies may travel back and forth between the different dimensions to achieve their objectives. Portals are popular with low-level energies such as lost souls, evil spirits and demonic entities. They grant trespassers easy access into our reality where they could embark on mischief before disappearing from whence they came.

The longer a portal is left unattended, the more established it becomes and therefore harder to close or seal. There are many techniques into handling the closure of a portal and I apply a basic procedure where I visualise a strong wire mesh at the opening and then I cover it with a golden white light. I continue to flood the area with white light and I hold the image in my mind's eye for as long as I can and then I place my hands on the physical surface (if there is one) where the portal is present and I transfer the feeling of closure. Finally, I close the session with a with a prayer to cleanse and to bless the surroundings.

Dealing with portals requires focus, it has to be dealt with swiftly so that there is the least amount of disturbance or intrusions from the other side, but they also have to be sealed so that the disturbance does not recur again and sealed in a manner where none of the intrusive energies that has crossed over using the portal are left behind.

Portals have wreaked havoc in people's lives. The most common mischief that entities get up to is to appear and be seen by at least one family member and then they vanish back into the portal, making it difficult for the remaining family members to believe the witness accounts. Should medium or psychics help, they are confused because they do not feel a presence of a spirit or an entity, unless they manage to detect the portal. Since it is an opening into another dimension, the expected and the unexpected may wander through into our dimension. Many lost souls who evaded going into the light after their passing find themselves crossing through portals into our world. Instead of returning to us, they become trapped between two worlds. Trapped souls need to be assisted and guided to help them cross into the light. This is usually achieved with the help of a medium who helps them recognise their situation and overcome their earthly times to help them to cross successfully.

I once attended to a portal at a family home but before closure, I scanned the perimeter with my mind's eye and saw a female spirit in the room. She was an older woman with a kind face and a quiet demeanour, she was in old fashion garments, an apron and head band. I sensed she had crossed into our world from the portal and she looked disoriented and nervous. I enquired about her presence and she said she wanted to help with the children of the family who I was attending to. I told her the children were doing fine, their mother and father were looking after them. She claimed her right to stay and stressed that she was needed in the house and just wanted to help. I explained she was scaring the family and it was time to go. After much communication back and forth, I understood she was terrified of crossing over because she feared death and losing her identity. Working with children was all she knew so I assured her there was plenty for her to do on the other side and there was nothing to fear; she wouldn't lose her identity. She did leave on her own accord, albeit reluctantly because she was just a lost soul and wanted to be somewhere she felt needed. She was harmless but still, her presence was detected by the family and she was affecting their peace of mind. I pray in her crossing, she has found the peace that she also deserves.

Nearly every lost soul I've dealt with is a sad story. They need comfort, reassurance and a lot of patience to eventually understand that their place is no longer here in our reality. Most have crossed over to the other side but are still attached to their earthly past, memories and loved ones. They need reassurance that they will be met with love when they go into the light, their true home. Some fear crossing over because they feel they will be punished in hell for their wrongs on earth. Others are convinced they are not dead because they did not meet an end as expected from their religious teachings. Most common is the fear of losing their. Their identity is the last bit of reality they can relate to and they fear if that is lost, then they are dispersed into oblivion.

We are all fragile even if we have crossed into the afterlife. I make sure to approach the poor souls with great care and tenderness. I send them healing thoughts of calm and I ask for the blessed angels to help guide them back home, into the light where they now belong.

EXORCISM

The word 'exorcism' is synonymous with the movie 'The Exorcist' and it invokes intense and dramatic images. We watched a demon torment the lives of a child and her family in the process of the demon taking over the child. We also saw the failed attempt by a couple Catholic priests who tried to exorcise the demon out of the girl at the cost of their own lives. Although it appeared the demon was cast out in the end, we were left with many questions. The movie was intense and powerful and invoked deep feelings in the audience. Warnings were posted at the entrances to cinemas where it was screened and some movie goers suffered emotionally, mentally and even physically. Some fainted while others went through serious panic attacks; it was not uncommon to see an ambulance parked outside theatres where the movie was being screened.

Although the movie had some impact on me at the time, I do not remember being particularly horrified or scared, I was indeed mystified. Could the situation in the movie ever occur in real life? What was to stop it from happening? Many such questions came to my mind.

My real-life experience in exorcism is both different and similar to what's seen in movies. It is extremely rare to witness Hollywood effects in real life exorcisms, the realization that what is happening is real can be even scarier than projectile vomiting or furniture being moved around. The volunteers and I feel a distinct drop in temperature and we all sense a shift in the energy and it feels colder and darker. The only thing that keeps the entities at bay is faith and even then, there are times when that alone is not enough. You have to call on your courage and be mentally focused and strong. The entities use many tactics to fail us by corrupting our minds with seeds of doubt and fear. Fear is the most prominent weapon used by the possessing entities, they scream, shout and threaten. They present formidable physical strength and excel at acting and performing, especially if they feel that they have a captive audience. At the start of a session, they will try to exploit any weakness in those present, mainly the exorcist. They will use pity and may even play the role of the victim to get sympathy and support. I ignore everything that I see and hear. My focus is on my patient and my service to God. The patients are entrusted to me, their lives are in my hand, I have to ensure that I do my absolute best and no less.

I am at the receiving end of threats that can be quite serious. I do not take exorcism lightly, I learnt to never underestimate any of the entities or their hosts. Anger and hate combined are powerful, far more powerful than we could possibly imagine. The bottom line is that the entities want us to fear, so that they can intimidate us into surrendering our beliefs and hopes. This is a true spiritual battle between good and bad and the entity's primary goal is to gain the upper hand. They will resort to anything and everything, including threats.

One day, an entity I was exorcising sent me a mental image of my daughter and then my wife. The entity impressed on me mentally in a menacing voice, "We can get them...."

I cannot deny that I was shaken by this threat, I was worried for a couple days. I later had a coffee with Doreen, a dear medium friend, and she picked up that I was hurting inside, so I told her about the message. She told me not to be bothered with it because it was meant to weaken me.

"Garo, should it ever happen again, tell them to piss off!"

When her message sank in, I realized that was absolutely right so I changed my approach. Nowadays when I am stung, I hit back harder and I tell the offending entity to shut up. The impact is effective since it is driven by faith and devotion but more so because it originates from someone who is not prepared to put up with nonsense. I am very protective of my patients and my family and I no longer react to threats from entities, I stand my ground, I have faith. Years of abuse, bullying and pain have taught me to be tough, especially in the face of bullies. Entities are bullies with a few extra tricks up their sleeves. The bottom line is that bullies can most certainly be brought to their knees, it is only a matter of time.

My favourite part of exorcism is when the possessing entity has been cast out and the patient is liberated from the dark energy. I see a distinct transformation in the features of the patient: the eyes, the colour in their face and sometimes they may even flash a smile I sit back and observe them coming to terms with the fact that their ordeal has come to an end. They usually look around in a daze, knowing that something has shifted, and their reaction is of awe, yet they still feel afraid that whatever it was will come back. I reassure them that it is gone and that it will not return. It is not uncommon for a patient to breakdown in tears at this stage so we comfort them very quietly. The journey to their recovery begins. I ask these patients to return for further examination in the future and we observe their behaviour to ensure they are now sufficiently improved and are able to carry themselves forward with their lives. They are usually confused about what to do next, so I refer them to their family and friends to help them readjust to their normal lives. In many cases, they will also be referred to a therapist for further help.

ATTACHMENTS

Energies, attachments and evil spirits are connected somehow or at least share a common element. Negative energy can affect patients as well as their household and others. In such situations, patients may even be unaware that they are spreading such energy until things get so bad that they can no longer be ignored.

Sometimes because of the nature of the curse or magic, it's more difficult to get to the bottom of the issue. It is not impossible but much harder than when tapping into an intelligent entity, for instance. A static energy needs to be investigated through a combination of psychic sense or intuition, logical thinking and communicating with the patient and those who are involved with him or her. Without guidance from the helpers, it would be impossible to succeed as facts can become muddled and forgotten. Also the patient usually cannot recall past events due to being drained and lacking focus in the first place.

Attachments are common. Some are just lost souls seeking company while others are malevolent creatures that serve a dark purpose. Most hosts are unaware of their uninvited parasites and explain their personal issues as normal parts of relationships, God's will or that they are paying for their sins. But sometimes strange things happen and the hosts understand that there is something externally, an independent intelligence that is affecting their lives or judgements and wellbeing. I have learnt that the attachments can be any number of possibilities, for example they could be human spirits that are lost or refusing to cross over to the other side. They somehow 'link' with hosts who may in some cases share similar qualities. Sometimes attachments find hosts that 'entertain' or 'amuse' them in a sadistic or twisted manner.

I once exorcised a mean spirit of an older gentleman who had attached himself to a gifted young man. He was having serious mood swings and outbursts and rage towards his mother. The mother had become a nervous wreck and lost control of the household which was slowly imploding as a result. When I tapped into the energy responsible, I could see that it was a male and I questioned his purpose behind attaching himself to the young man. Although the attachment didn't answer my questions, I sensed he was there to entertain himself at the expense of the son and mother fighting each other over trivial matters, most of which were issues that he instigated. He was nasty and certainly deserved no place in their lives. He was dealt with eventually and left the poor young man. An immediate change could be seen on the young man's face. He looked peaceful and his eyes changed from being spiteful to kind. He beamed with a large, warm and loving smile.

In recent years, I've observed the number of attachments is on the rise, and most hosts are unaware of the intrusion until the attachment has a direct impact on their lives. Some attachments operate stealthily, making subtle changes while others may be more forceful in getting what they want from their hosts. Others are particularly cautious if a host is sensitive or intuitive and in these cases they will do their best to remain undetected for as long as conditions allow.

If not dealt with, attachments may well develop into far more serious issues. They specifically seek out the weak, the vulnerable and the troubled. Usually they prefer to operate stealthily in the background, making sure their host is unaware of their presence. However, there are occasions when attachments do communicate by influencing the host's thoughts or decision making process. Some believe that a large number of people who appear to be mentally ill and talking to themselves or displaying various inexplicable behaviour may be misdiagnosed.

Every patient I've worked with who suffered with an attachment has said he or she felt something was interfering with their thoughts and identity and causing confusion. Most of them felt they were losing their minds and kept matters secretive to avoid being labelled crazy. Many felt that their actions were not their own and they were being influenced to behave in a certain manner which conflicted with their constitution and morals. I fully understand the strategy behind the dark attachments and why they choose to make their 'victims' resent their own actions; to make them hate themselves. The more we hate ourselves the further we are from God.

Needless to say, there are cases where it is quite obvious that someone's behaviour becomes inexplicable and exaggerated. Most of the hosts whose behaviour is influenced directly by their attachments cannot justify or explain their actions. For instance, a host may become addicted to gambling, drinking or drugs, a behaviour not usually associated with him or her. The darker the attachment, the darker the behaviour of the host. Many murders have been committed by individuals who later claimed that they were unaware of their actions or had no control over themselves. Of course there are many hard-core evil criminals who will use any excuse to justify their crimes but I am referring to the ordinarily good people who have committed serious crimes that do not fit their personality or character.

Modern society confines criminals to prison and society almost forgets about them; out of sight, out of mind. I believe that there should be further and deeper research conducted into why perfectly 'normal' people can snap all of a sudden and engage in the darkest of acts. If, after rigorous testing, it is determined that the criminal was not driven due to logical or scientific reason then there could be a possibility to assume that the driving force may have been paranormal in nature. Labelling perpetrators as 'bad' or 'evil' is not sufficient to simply file them away without adequate insight into the driving force behind their acts. There must be a reason behind their actions and sometimes the truth gets ignored because it is right before our eyes.

I sincerely look forward to the day when deeper and more meaningful studies are conducted in order to better understand the real triggers behind some of our negative or darker behaviour. I believe that this is a large and unchartered chapter in humanity that is yet to be fully understood. Perhaps, when we gain better insight into the real reasons for the triggers behind some of these criminal acts, we may then evolve and find better ways in dealing with humanity's darker side and in consequence, strive towards a brighter future.

Unfortunately, the systems at present are influenced by creeds that make it impossible for non-scientific possibilities to be considered. It is somewhat ironic that the countries that reject the idea of investigating other possibilities follow religious ideology and implement it into law. Maybe one day, new possibilities may be considered but until then, I personally can only do what I can do to help remove attachments from those who seek my help. Sadly, the number of cases is growing exponentially, and the associated darkness grows stronger every day.

I become concerned when I can feel a presence and yet am unable to home in on the source. Sometimes I feel that I am being shielded from being exposed to danger and that my work is being deliberately postponed to a time when the entity and the removal process is more manageable. Maybe the process requires both myself and the patient to be aligned somehow and linked in a manner that enables me to deal with the entity with the least amount of interference from the patient. I know now that the more a patient is defensive during the clearance session the less is accomplished. When the patient surrenders him or herself, the clearance process is vastly improved and a lot more is achieved.

There is no guide book when it comes to exorcism or clearing attachments. I rely on my gut instinct and faith. I begin each exorcism by visualising the crucifix and I mentally superimpose that image over the patient at all times. This gives me assurance and strength that we will prevail. Also, different prayers are recited according to different religions, but this battle is not won by prayer alone. No one can foresee the direction or the outcome of the exorcism. It is a test of nerves and faith and the entities will do their best to push the exorcist to the limit and beyond. My faith is my strength and I do feel responsible for all my patients and that I have to protect them. When the battle commences, I never think of the consequences, my focus is on how to address the unwanted entity. In my mind, I know that God's will shall always prevail and despite all threats, screams or parlour tricks, the entity is defeated even prior to the start of the process. The fact that the patient is seeking help is a good indication that there is hope and hope is powerful.

I have heard of patients visiting other exorcists and later complain that the symptoms return, and they feel something negative within them or around them once again. The experience does leave a scar that needs to be addressed and healed. Even if an entity has been exorcised and has been removed from its host, there remains the shattered pieces of the hosts' lives, their healing will need time, it is also recommended that they seek professional help from a therapist or counsellor as well.

DETECTION

I do not have a set formula on how I detect the presence of an attachment or attachments (there are instances where patients may have more than one). Initially, I may have a gut instinct after observing certain characteristics and behaviour. The eyes also are a giveaway. People with attachments tend to be uncomfortable with eye contact with me. This does not mean that everyone who does not make eye contact with me necessarily has an attachment but such are the tell-tale signs that alert me to the fact that something is not quite right with the person. Usually the hosts or patients are oblivious to the fact that their eyes express far more than they are aware of. A host may be a nice person with a charming smile but unknown to them a reaction of some sort may escape them for a fleeting second and immediately the alarm bells will ring. I follow my gut instinct seriously so even if I do not visually see anything that immediately raises concern, I will never ignore my feelings. There are also other physical signs to watch out for such as out of place smiles and strange facial expressions or a long and eerie cold stare. I usually observe the patient without them knowing to look for these signs among others. These signs do not always necessarily indicate the presence of an attachment. Patients may be suffering from anxiety or some form of psychophysical disturbance or even mental illness. This is why trusting my gut instinct and good observation are paramount.

When I detect the presence of an attachment in a patient, I try to engage him in conversation to collect some facts and evidence to back my feelings. During the process of the patient describing their issues, I usually try to tap into the attachment energy to see if I can feel anything from it. I do this prior to the commencement of the actual process of clearing the attachment so that I can try and gain some knowledge or insight and try to be a step ahead. It does not work all the time but it occasionally does and it is of great help. Sometimes, hosts relay information from their attachments without me having to ask for it. It is as if the attachment somehow was expecting the clearing session and goes on the offence. They supply misleading and confusing information in the hope that the host's credibility is questioned and the session is brought to a close. It is not very common but when it occurs, I am eventually guided to the truth even when I am intentionally misled.

I usually start by putting the patient at ease and I explain my findings to so that they understand fully what is going on. I describe their feelings and some of their experiences so that they can be assured that I have actually linked with them. I open with a prayer and the first signs start to show in the facial expression and frequently inexplicable sobbing from the host. I am not quite sure why they cry, I sometimes think that maybe it is because they realize that their time with the host has come to an end or perhaps even the fact that they realize that they will be moving away from the earth plane. Whatever it is, I do not pay attention. I do not follow set rules, I just go along with my feelings and the guidance from my helpers. At first, I do not visualise anything but sit in silence with my hand on the patient's hand and I wait for the attachment to reveal itself. This is the waiting game and I have to be patient, sometimes I feel it is similar to fishing, when you cast the line and wait. Who knows what you will reel in eventually but the wait is worthwhile. Sometimes, it does not take long before something emerges but the majority of times, it is a waiting game.

When the entity reveals itself, I see it in my mind's eye but I may also may catch glimpses of it with my naked eye. They seem to always appear from behind the host's shoulder or just in front of it and nearer to their chest, just below the neck area. When I am able to see the entity, then I know that the clearing will commence and it is countdown until its extraction and dismissal. I go deeper into nothingness, I stop all thought and focus on the image of a crucifix with a bright light behind it and I say a prayer. I superimpose the image of the crucifix on the patient and surround the patient's back and sides with the white light. At this stage the entity is unaware that I have surrounded the patient with light and that it is now trapped. The only way out leads to me directly which is the very position I want it to be in. I usually feel the energy flowing through me, making its way to the patient and eventually I visualise a clear channel and try to communicate with the entity to hear what it has to say for itself. Usually, they volunteer information in different formats for example by audible speech, visual imagery and other sensations. Some are only too happy to divulge information about themselves and why they are there, while others choose to remain silent. There are those who issue threats, some serious ones. There are occasions when the entity may even change their shape and appearance, sometimes even pretend that it is more than one entity while in fact it is one alone. The shape-shifters as I call them are the trickiest that I have dealt with and have managed to confuse me on several occasions. I would start by a mental image of the entity and then I find a different entity in my vision but I realize that it is the same entity, it just changed its position or vibration to make it harder for me to tune into it. I pull back and try to tune in again but this time, I surround it and bound it with light. The one thing that the entities are unable to do is to avoid detection, I always feel their presence and they always react to mine. Sometimes it may take longer but in the end we always succeed by the grace of God.

I listen to what the entity has to say to distract it and gather information, but I never accept or believe it, I certainly do not sympathize. It is not the victim. It is quite remarkable that in most cases where patients are female, their attachments have been of male energies and the majority are nearly always sexually motivated. I once worked on a female patient who had suffered for a long time from an inexplicable feeling of darkness in her life. I tuned in and saw that it was an older male energy, he told me that he had no intention of leaving her. I picked up that he was perversely 'enjoying' her, he sent me images of her having baths, when she was drying herself and putting on her clothes. Sexuality is quite common as a drive when it comes to entities choosing their hosts, it is not uncommon for some hosts to be influenced or inspired to engage in sexual acts that would not ordinarily be befitting of their character or sexual preferences. Attachments can successfully manoeuvre and guide their hosts to engage in all manners of self-harming activities such as gambling, drinking, drugs, etc. Attachments that have been failures in their earthly lives or in their previous incarnations particularly enjoy seeing others fail, especially those of us who are successful or even with hopes and aspirations. They affect our moods and emotions, they are expert manipulators.

Some attachments are demonic in nature and these present a far more sinister and dangerous purpose. It is not uncommon for such forces to try and push their hosts to much darker levels and try to influence them to commit various atrocities, such as murder or rape for instance. The prisons are full of people who ordinarily are incapable of such crimes and yet they do commit them and later most of them claim that they have no recollection of what led them to it. Many will say that they almost 'observed' themselves in the process of hurting others but were unable to stop themselves from doing so. I am not a psychologist, nor am I a criminologist. I do feel that this behaviour and condition needs to be explored and not simply dismissed as a psychological or mental issue. There are many inmates in prisons around the world who were once good people but inexplicably find themselves committing or getting involved in serious crimes that lead to their incarcerations. Most of them claim not to have control over themselves and 'blanking out' during their criminal episodes. Of course I am not in any way implying that criminal activity is justifiable, far from it. However, I do believe that there may well be a proportion of people who are driven into criminal activity by an external influence. It is too convenient to dismiss the common theme of them being unaware of what they were doing at the time. This condition deserves closer scrutiny and we do need to investigate it to learn more about why humans behave this way and the best preventative measures.

Demonic energies are hard to combat but are not impossible to defeat. This level of work requires more time, faith and absolute trust in my helpers on the other side. I have to feel safe, otherwise I cannot let go of myself. Even though I deal with unknown energies and entities that are dark in nature, I still feel protected. I am blessed with helpers on the other side but also on this side of life. The volunteers who help me, Linda, Marie, Alabama and Jane radiate an exceptional energy of love and peace, it is humbling and reassuring.

Nevertheless, despite all assurances, I would be a fool to underestimate any of the entities and so I make sure that my earthly helpers and volunteers and I are all sufficiently protected and we follow strict procedures. These entities may try to intimidate me using fear and other distractions, which I expect but I try to focus on the task. I usually do not have any prior knowledge of the entity, who it is and what it wants until the start of the process. I have to rely on my instincts, psychic or otherwise, and communication from my helpers to be informed about what I am dealing with. Regardless of how things unfold, I have to be in control and be strong for everybody's sake, especially the patients who rely on me and trust me with their fates. I cannot show weakness to any energy, attachment or entity, I have to be strong. Maybe it also helps that I am stubborn by nature, who knows. What I do know is that I have a very strong sense of justice and responsibility for my patients, especially if we link and a bond is formed between us.

With the entity contained and bound in white light, I offer it to leave peacefully and quietly. Sometimes they may do so without a fight but generally they refuse to leave, so I call on for assistance from the other side and I start the extraction process using prayer and visualisation. Visualisation is a big part of my service and I find myself able to do it even when my eyes are open, and I stay focused on the images projected.

Once the work begins, it has to be seen through to the end. I may not always emerge as the winner, nobody can, but I do make sure that I always deliver my best. In the process, I try to focus on protecting the patient from whatever is troubling them so that the patient is empowered and regains some control over his or her life. As we make progress in rebutting the entity, the fight becomes harder and the entity more elusive. It is not uncommon for me to suddenly feel ill or nauseous and quite often disorientation and inexplicably drained. I have observed that after the entity is successfully dealt with, all symptoms that I experienced during the process would disappear and I regain my composure once again. It is not uncommon for dark or evil entities to physically attack the healer or exorcist and they are by far physically much stronger and at a greater advantage.

There is no way of knowing how long the session will last. It will go on for as long as is required for the energy to be cleared from the patient. In most cases, this may require several sessions, and some will be more intense than others. Eventually, after the exorcism, there is a distinct change in the hosts' demeanour and facial expressions. No more cold and angry stares, no more incoherent babbling, they look peaceful and human, in command of their lives again. They have returned to themselves.

It took years for me to be accepted into this realm because I had to be aptly prepared to help others. It is a huge responsibility and people are trusting me with their lives or the lives of their loved ones. I had to sort out my personal issues and confront my own demons before tackling other people's conflicts. Along the way, I gave up many times, desperate to find a way to fit into society and to conform to a mainstream lifestyle, but I was never happy when away from service. It was always a struggle for me to be away from my parents and siblings in Lebanon, but I had no choice. My service dictated that I should be in London where I am accepted in a society that understands and appreciates the significance of those who are gifted. It is a shame that throughout the world, there are many gifted individuals who are born into cultures that may not accept them for who they are and so their gifts are suppressed. I hope that one day, more cultures and societies embrace and accept gifted individuals and value what they can do. Unfortunately what does not help, is the fact that there are many individuals who abuse their gifts or are plainly scam artists and they compromise the trust put in them from patients and others. The gift is not a bartering tool, nor is it to be profited from financially or materially. The gift is pure and should be guarded as such, it is love that drives the helpers to help us and love should be what drives us to serve our fellow man.

My communicator made it clear that I was never to charge any amount or to accept any gifts for my service. I have observed this diligently and turned down many offers; I have never charged a single penny for my service, even when I was in dire need of money. I have always trusted in my communicator's wise words

"You look after others and you will always be looked after yourself...."

HAUNTED HOUSES

It is always challenging to deal with hauntings of any nature, especially haunted houses which I prefer to refer to as houses with a 'disturbance'. A haunting is usually very intense and intimidating for the residents and sometimes downright terrifying. Some households feel that it is best not to allow an exorcist into their home, fearing that it may make their situation worse. I fully understand their position.

It takes a lot of trust and reassurance before attempting a clearance. The situation must be approached with care and caution because of the unknown origins of the hauntings. The disturbance could be a call for help by a distressed soul, seeking attention or recognition or it could be a malevolent entity who is having a field day at the family's expense by terrorising them. We cannot know for sure until the process of detecting and clearing is started. I have to expect the unexpected and stay in control of my feelings and anxiety. It would be foolish to approach hauntings without a sensible degree of caution. It is finding the right balance between courage and fear and acknowledging both. Before starting the process, I may interact with the residents of the house for information that could help me. I listen to their stories and try to find out about the history of the house and some of their experiences. I enquire with the residents about the number of years they've lived at the property and any other information such as their interest in the paranormal or occult and their family backgrounds. The more information the residents volunteer, the better are the chances at restoring peace to the house. I do not rule out the possibility that I may be lied to, it has happened before. People try to hide sensitive aspects of their lives, especially embarrassing mistakes by being economical with the truth. This makes the situation more difficult and complicated but not impossible to deal with because eventually the truth will emerge. I was once invited to a home with a disturbance and I started my enquiries with the family and each one recounted their own version of events. None of them told me that a certain member of the family had been in close contact with a sorcerer for whatever reason, nor was I told that items of clothing tarnished with blood were given to this family member to store in the house. I found it very bizarre that this information was not shared with me, because it explained quite a lot about what was going on. I tried to address the issue with the person concerned but they were in denial, despite being warned of consequences. There was little that could be achieved in clearing the disturbance unless the subject of the bloodied clothes and related were discussed openly and honestly. Seeing how the information was not forthcoming, I decided it best to move on and leave it up to the residents of the house to decide if they seriously want to bring matters to an end.

Once I feel that I have gathered enough information and I am ready to begin, I start the clearing process by taking a step back from the residents of the house so that I am not distracted or overwhelmed by them. I try to tune in to the disturbance. I have to remain subjective and focused so that I can tune in to the problem with the least amount of interference.

The clearance of hauntings depends on intuition and some detective work to some degree to determine if there are any helpful hints that could point me in the right direction. Disturbances occur for a reason and unless the root of the problem is addressed and treated, the issue will persist. Even if armed with knowledge and a full clear picture I can never be complacent or assume that I will always emerge a winner. I have absolute faith and trust in my helpers, but I do remind myself that in all experiences there are lessons to be learnt. Sometimes, people have to go through certain difficulties to learn and hauntings are no different.

Not all 'haunted' houses are necessarily inhabited by something 'evil'. In many cases, the activity which is seen as a 'disturbance' may be due to a restless spirit that is trying to convey a message or to reveal something, as in the case of a murder scene for instance A kindred spirit, a suicide or a victim of abuse may also be attempting to convey a message. In these cases, the approach has to be very delicate and I do my best to ease the restless soul so that I can help it. If the matter is complicated and beyond me, I call on my helpers to assist and I may even surrender the process to the blessed angels so that they can ease the restless soul into the light.

I recall on one occasion I was invited to a 'haunted' house to help a troubled family. My friend and gifted medium Marie, who was with me at the time, pinpointed the origin of the disturbance to a room in the loft. We went up there together and we both felt strange in that room. I closed my eyes to focus and sense what the origin of the disturbance was. Soon an entity revealed itself. It refused to leave and I could tell that it was powerful. Before long, I saw another entity next to the one I was dealing with and I could feel their energy overpowering me. I wasn't sure if it was a single entity playing tricks or if it was two entities and I started to feel at a disadvantage because of my confusion. I took a breath, and shut myself down and then I lined the doorway to the loft with a bright white light. I was relaying this information to Marie and I asked her to protect herself After a while, it became clear to me that it was in fact one entity and it was trying to confuse us and distract us. I kept visualising the white light getting stronger and surrounding the entity so that in fact it became trapped. It refused to communicate at first but eventually when it did, I saw an older man, stern like a headmaster type. He refused to leave and said I should not waste his time or mine. I asked him who granted him authority to be in the house and why he was disturbing the family. He was in the house before the family moved in and felt he had a right to be there. I was receiving images and visions in relation to this entity in parallel to its communication. Even though I do not usually engage with entities, I prodded him for answers.

It turns out that he soon became interested in the lady of the house who is a gifted psychic herself and eventually this turned to some form of a sexual obsession. He would watch her and try to get her attention but he was blocked from taking things further so he became angry and his anger rose by the day because he felt excluded. She was his 'property' as far as he was concerned, he did not want to share her with others, not even her daughters. Eventually he went on a rampage, declaring war on her daughters by terrifying them. He was a master shape-shifter and physically materialized on occasion in different guises to try and scare the family. His intention was to punish the daughters and to push them away from their mother and to isolate the mother so that eventually he could form a deeper link with her.

I stood at the doorway to prevent him from coming out and before I even had a chance to go through the process, I was interrupted by my communicator who told me, "Leave him to us, he is much too dangerous for you." I came out of the light trance and returned back to myself. I was blocked for my own protection. When the energy was cleared, we all felt a noticeable difference in the air and we were delighted. I briefed the lady of the house on my findings and what had occurred and she was shocked to hear of this revolting creature. I was to later understand that the entity's speciality was illusion and distraction. It would have affected my mind and successfully compromised me had I not been disconnected from its energy.

All disturbances have ceased in that house and the family now enjoys a loving relationship.

CURSES, SPELLS AND MAGIC

A significant proportion of patients who visit me and are victims of curses, spells or magic. The practice of employing magic or sorcery is quite prevalent in the African subcontinent, Asia and the Middle East. The service of putting a spell or a curse on someone is openly available in many countries where for a certain fee, a sorcerer performs the necessary rituals for the spell or curse to take effect. The more complicated or difficult the request by the client, the higher the fees requested by the sorcerer and the bigger the demands by the conjured entities who do the sorcerer's bidding.

This type of magic requires cooperation and association with entities from the dark side who the sorcerer serves by desecrating religious items or sacrificing creatures or even humans in extreme cases if necessary. This is performed in anticipation of a reward by said low level entities who usually fulfil their part of the deal based on the sorcerer's delivery. If possible, personal items from the intended victim, such as hair, finger nails, photos, etc. are made available to the sorcerer who will use them in the ritual. Providing physical ingredients from the intended victim is integral to the ritual because a physical link or 'hook' is established and firmly locked in place. This is what makes the removal of curses or spells more difficult because the magic becomes embedded within the victim's psyche as well as their physical body, even without having contact with the sorcerer. The link is established remotely and somehow it may even manifest on the victim physically in the form of inexplicable marks on their body that lead to no conclusion when inspected by a medical professional.

The spells and curses are effective and I have witnessed the suffering caused on people as a consequence. Depending on what result is being aimed for, in the case of a destructive spell or curse, the effects can be extremely debilitating. I have even heard of cases where this practice has eventually led to the death of the victim. Some patients may have prior knowledge of this sinister practice and they may be aware that they are under the influence of a curse and even suspect who may be responsible. Other patients may not even be aware that whatever they are suffering from is a direct result of the dark practice.

In cultures where the dark practice is common, victims end up visiting different sorcerers or religious figures to try to remove the curse. Prayers may help but rarely become effective without divine intervention because of the complexity and power of the curse. The magic employed is a science in its own right and few can understand its mechanics without becoming involved in sorcery and the dark art. To counter the effect of the curse, the different sorcerer in consultation with entities, will attempt to first identify the source of the curse and the person responsible. Usually the investigating sorcerer will provide names of people involved with descriptions and this assures the victim that they are on the right path. At this stage the sorcerer will ask the victim for money and other 'gifts' for the entities (gold coins, silver, etc...) and may also ask for a personal item from the victim to establish a link. The victim is sent away and the sorcerer commences his rituals. Not much is known about what the sorcerer does in private as it is a closely guarded secret but I had visions of the sorcerer going into a semi-conscious state with mantras and prayers, incense, candles and chants. These are designed to conjure up his own entities and he communicates the requirements to them and he makes the offerings in returns. The entities are entrusted in disabling the original curse using their powers and influences. The darker the entities, the more powerful and effective that they can be and so the more of a chance that they will be successful in the removal of the curse. It is in effect using dark practice to counter another dark practice.

Unfortunately for the victims, no part of the process is guaranteed to end successfully. There is also the risk that the sorcerer may not even truthful and may pocket the money and gifts and ask for more money and favours in return for doing deeper and more effective rituals. Desperate victims willingly part with their material possessions in the hope that something, anything can be done to help them. It is not unheard of for females to be coaxed into surrendering themselves sexually to sorcerers who convince them that it will be an ultimate act of sacrifice to please the entities.

Some parts of the world are synonymous with this dark practice. Charms, spells and curses are openly sold on the streets, in shops and in private. Some countries are picturesque and tourist attractions and although we would love to visit the sights and enjoy their beautiful beaches, I have always told my wife that we should not go for this reason. A few years ago, there was a call to Arab men, specifically from the Gulf states, to avoid visiting a certain Arabic speaking North African country. Many men have gone there to enjoy female company and fun but end up becoming alienated from their own families and walking away from their wives and children back home in a short space of time. The men were found to be settling with new partners and many got married in a short space of time. The high numbers of sudden and inexplicable transformations led to investigation which uncovered that many of the men were being manipulated through magic and sorcery. At least one Gulf state took this issue seriously and were considering their options, even if it meant issuing a travel ban to the country in question.

The dark practice is prevalent in many different cultures and societies. It may be referred to as black magic, sorcery, witchcraft, magic, etc. They are all one and the same but operate differently from one another.

Many patients have come into the church seeking help for symptoms that they could not attribute to specific conditions. Some of them may have suffered for years and did everything that they could to find a remedy or a resolution to their problem until one way or another they ended up at the church out of sheer desperation. I ask all new patients not to tell me of their conditions as I prefer to feel things myself. This way I can relay to the patient what I am picking up and the patient can be assured that what they are receiving is genuine because I was not informed beforehand. In the case of a spell, curse or magic, it becomes much harder because we are not dealing with a an external intelligence that is directly connected to the patient such as an entity. Energy in its raw format is inanimate, meaning that it does not necessarily respond as an intelligent entity would. The magic is conducted using symbols and vague characters, even if I was to see them, I will still need to work out how to disable the curse. Sometimes, I feel who the curse originated from and I share this information with the patient to assure them that we are on the right track. Since the curse is made up of symbols and energy, I found that I could tune into it using different methods to be able to assist the patient.

I once worked with a man suffering terribly from the effect of a black magic spell. It was my first experience in dealing with this sort of thing. During the healing process, I saw a specific symbol and it kept coming back to my mind despite me pushing it to the side and trying to focus on the patients. Then, I received communication that the man was under a curse and I was told of his condition. He could hardly use his hands and even his walking and daily functions were affected. It was hard work as I had to be guided on what to do but slowly we started getting closer to the truth and we established who was the culprit behind his pain. The question remained, how to remove or disable the curse, I really had no idea.

I stopped the healing and I explained my position to the patient as well as the volunteers. I was seeing an abstract image or a symbol of the curse, but I am unsure what to do to remove it. It was the patient who helped shed light on the situation when he casually contributed,

"If it is an abstract symbol, then perhaps you need to use an abstract technique to deal with it."

He was absolutely right and it made sense. I took a break and closed my eyes and used visualisation and symbolic images to counter the curse and with the help of someone closely related to the patient in spirit, the curse was eventually removed. But it took time an incredible amount of focus. I had to maintain the images in my head while making sure my mind was focused on the symbol at all times. It required concentration and a strong will because I had to will the symbol to change and impose a new image on it all the while retaining the image clearly. It help that I was relaxed and in a semi-conscious state of mind. Eventually, it was as if I was watching a television screen inside my head and changes were occurring quite independent of me.

Once the symbol's appearance was altered and eventually compromised, I felt that this was the end; the curse has been rendered ineffective. I prayed and then sealed the patient with white light and then I told him that it was over. Before I had told him, one of my team commented about how the patient's face had already changed and was glowing. He expressed delight and was grateful. I asked him to return the next week and we were all surprised how totally different he looked—thinner, younger, eyes sparkling and a smile on his face; he was alive!

He showed me how he was able to use his hand where he had been almost paralysed previously.

There was great joy on that day and ours was even greater than the patient's.

It is sad that many people resort to the dark practices to achieve their ambitions. Money, love, sex and power are top on the list but equally high are revenge curses and spells. Causing harm to others in retaliation for whatever reason is in great demand. What puzzles me is the fact that people can put their trust in a total stranger, a sorcerer, to do harm on to others and not think twice about the possibility that the sorcerer could possibly turn on them and do them harm. I have heard of cases where sorcerers harm their clients and demand more rewards to help release them from curses which they blame on other sorcerers.

In some parts of the world where this sort of activity is rampant, capital punishment has been introduced as a deterrent and several sorcerers have been arrested and some were executed. In some Arabian countries, the governments have setup specialist task forces, usually accompanied by religious figures who supervise the disabling of charms, curses or spells after sorcerers are captured. Videos of such cases and arrests are available for viewing on various online platforms. Despite all drastic measures and consequences, the dark practice shows no decline, it is in fact on the rise and attracts more nationalities and religions than ever before.

Since then, I have dealt with others who are suffering from similar issues and by the grace of God and His blessed angels, all have successfully been liberated of the poison.

Printed in Great Britain
by Amazon